SPIRITUAL MAXIMS

Stepping Stones to Sanctity.

by John Nicholas Grou, S.J.

(1731 – 1803)

CONTENTS

Translator's Preface

According to the French Jesuit Cadres, the Caracteres de la vraie devotion of Pere Grou - a work which ran into no less than forty- four editions - was first published in Paris in the year 1788. This was quickly followed by a further work on the same subject, but treated from a somewhat different and more practical angle, the Maximes Spirituelles avec des explications, published in the following year. In his Preface to the original edition, reproduced here in its place, the author says: 'At the end of the little work which I wrote on the Marks of true devotion, I promised to write another under the title of Spiritual Maxims, in which I would explain in more detail the means for practising that devotion. The following work is the result'. The former book defined what true devotion is: its motives, its object and the means for acquiring it; the second outlined in greater detail, as he says, the means for practising that devotion, always bearing in mind that, in Pere Grou's use of the word, devotion stands for the interior life or the life of the spirit.

The author's own life, being sufficiently known from his other works published in the Orchard Series it is hardly necessary to repeat all those details here. After the suppression of the Society of Jesus in France in the year 1763, and subsequently in Lorraine on the death of Duke Stanislaus in 1766, Pere Grou returned to Paris at the invitation of Mgr. de Beaumont, the Archbishop of Paris, and lived in seclusion and real poverty, under the name of Le Clerc, in a garret in the Rue de Sevres, occupying himself with study and writing, and with the direction of a community of Benedictine nuns nearby. It was at this time, roughly about the year 1767, that occurred what he always described as his 'conversion', through the instrumentality of a Visitation nun in the convent of the Rue du Bac, which was to have a profound influence on him for the rest of his life. For reasons which are not too clear, and for a period which is also uncertain, he appears to have passed some time in Holland, returning again to Paris, where he resumed the same life of simplicity, poverty and retirement as before, devoting himself almost exclusively to his personal sanctification and to the writing of books on the spiritual life. In the words of Pere Bernard, the writer of the article on Pere Grou in the Dictionnaire de Theologie Catholique, 'then commenced the series of magnificent treatises of a spirituality at once gentle and firm, penetrating and lofty, which place Pere Grou among the most eminent and best-beloved masters of the interior life'. I Of the works he produced at this time, the Maxims are, in the opinion of some, among his best. A contemporary critic says of this work: 'Few spiritual works contain more illuminating and profound rules for the guidance of the conscience and of the interior life'.

The title of this work recalls - perhaps intentionally the equally famous work of Fenelon, the Explications des Maximes des Saints, published in 1697 and condemned, after a fierce and not very edifying controversy with Bossuet, by Pope Innocent XII two years later. It is this unfortunate incident Pere Grou is referring to in his twenty-third Maxim; and, although the controversy did in fact die down, there is no doubt that there remained a certain element of uneasiness which lasted some time, and which was calculated for some considerable period to discredit even the true teaching of spiritual writers on the subject of prayer, and especially interior prayer. It was with this in mind that our author wrote (p. 252): 'As this subject, which is the highest of all relating to the interior life, caused much public comment at the end of the seventeenth century, and in consequence of a just condemnation many persons became prejudiced against a subject understood by very few, I have thought fit to explain the matter briefly, in order to correct certain false impressions, and to dispel prejudice'. So vivid, however, was the memory of Quietism and its condemnation that even Pere Grou, writing the best part of a century later, was not without his critics at the time. He himself admits that these matters are 'extremely delicate and very difficult to explain, or even to understand with perfect precision' (p. 251).

Pere Grou's great theme in the Spiritual Maxims is his insistence on the following of the spirit of Christ as opposed to what he calls the natural spirit, or the spirit of private judgment. Prayer for him is contemplative prayer, or the prayer of the interior way. Not that he despised formal meditation by any means, but he regarded it always as a stepping-stone towards a higher form of prayer, the intimate prayer of the spirit. His great aim and desire was to urge and encourage souls not to be afraid, but to persevere in a wholehearted gift of themselves to God, and in a faithful surrender to the guidance of the Holy Spirit.

The question has been asked: for whom is Pere Grou primarily writing, or whom had he in mind when he wrote his treatises on prayer, and especially the Spiritual Maxims? He himself says (p. 211) he is writing for beginners. This may be true of certain points, but in general one is inclined to think that some progress will need to have been made in the way of interior prayer if one is to appreciate, and profit by, his wise guidance. Still, there is something for more than one class of persons, we venture to think. Fr. Clarke, S.J., in his short Introduction to Pere Grou's How to Pray, expresses the belief that these writings (and one may apply the remark to the present work as well) should be a source of comfort and encouragement to many a disconsolate soul that has long struggled against aridity and desolation in prayer, and enable many whose prayers have hitherto been imperfect and ill- directed, to pray better. The influence of this book, in spite of the fact that it has only once been translated into English, persists to the present day. It is significant that Pere Grou was among the favourite spiritual writers of the late Abbot Chapman, and the Maxims was the only book, apart from his breviary, that he took with him to the nursing home where he died.

We have said that the Spiritual Maxims have only once been translated into English. This translation was issued from St. Margaret's Convent, East Grinstead, in the year 1874, and was published by J.T. Hayes of Eaton Square and Covent Garden, London. It ran into several editions, the sixth (by Thomas Baker, then of Newman Street, London) being published in 1924. This sixth edition--the one probably known to most readers of Grou--is identical in every way, even to the type, with the first edition, and is in fact a reprint of it.

It has generally been assumed that this translation was the work of the famous Anglican translator of hymns, the Rev. Dr. J.M. Neale, but this is at least extremely doubtful. Apart from the fact that Dr. Neale died in 1866, there is no reference to it among his works mentioned in the Dictionary of National Biography, nor is it recognized as his at the Convent itself. From an examination of the style, moreover, it would appear to be uneven, suggesting that it may well have been the work of more than one hand. However that may be, with the permission of Mr. Baker, it has been utilized to a certain extent by the present translator, although it soon became evident that a new and revised translation, following much more closely the original text, was needed. Even so, occasionally the over-long sentences favoured at the time have been curtailed, without, we hope, losing anything of the author's meaning; whilst much that was omitted in the 1874 translation has, with profit, been restored.

The paragraph on frequent communion in the sixth Maxim (p. 74) has been brought into line with the more recent directives on the subject by Pope St Pius X. Some obvious errors in the French text have been corrected; occasionally a few words have been added or omitted or even modified on account of certain obscurities in the original text, which could be misconstrued, contrary, we feel sure, to the author's intention. A list of all such corrections and amendments is given in the Notes at the end of this volume. At the request of the publishers, an article on Pere Grou from the pen of Baron Friedrich von Huegel, which appeared in The Tablet in December 1889, and which is well worth preserving in a more permanent form, has been added as an Appendix. Finally, a list, as complete as we have been able to make it, of the works of Pere Grou in French and in English translations, is given at the end.

St Hugh's Charterhouse,

Parkminster,

First Maxim: The Knowledge of God and the knowledge of self

By the ladder of sanctity, men ascend and descend at the same time.

All Christian sanctity is contained in two things: the knowledge of God, and the knowledge of self. 'Lord, that I may know Thee' cried St. Augustine, 'and that I may know myself'. A short prayer, but one opening out on to an infinite horizon. The knowledge of God elevates the soul; knowledge of self keeps it humble. The former raises the soul to contemplate something of the depths of the divine perfections, the latter lowers it to the abyss of its own nothingness and sin. [1] The amazing thing is that the very knowledge of God which raises man up, at the same time humbles him by the comparison of himself with God. Similarly self-knowledge, while it humbles him, lifts him up by the very necessity of approaching God in order to find solace in his misery.

Marvellous ladder of sanctity, whereon men descend even as they ascend. For the true elevation of man is inseparable from his true humiliation. The one without the other is pride, while the latter without the former is to be unhappy without hope. Of what use would be the most sublime knowledge of God to us, if the knowledge of ourselves did not keep us little in our own eyes? Similarly, would we not fall into terrible despair, if the knowledge of our exceeding meanness and misery were not counterbalanced by our knowledge of God? But this two-fold knowledge serves to sanctify us. To be a saint, we must know and admit that we are nothing of ourselves, that we receive all things from God in the order of nature and grace, and that we expect all things from Him in the order of glory.

By the knowledge of God, I do not mean abstract and purely ideal knowledge such as was possessed by pagan philosophers, who lost their way in vain and barren speculations, the only effect of which was to increase their pride. For the Christian, the knowledge of God is not an endless course of reasoning as to His essence and perfections, such as that of a mathematician concerned with the properties of a triangle or circle. There have been many philosophers and even theologians who held fine and noble ideas of God, but were none the more virtuous or holy as a result of it. The knowledge we must have is what God Himself has revealed concerning the Blessed Trinity; the work of each of the Persons in creating, redeeming and sanctifying us. We must know the scope of His power, His providence, His holiness, His justice and His love. We must know the extent and multitude of His mercies, the marvellous economy of His grace, the magnificence of His promises and rewards, the terror of His warnings and the rigour of His chastisements; the worship He requires, the precepts He imposes, the virtues He makes known as our duty, and the motives by which He incites us to their practice. In a word, we must know what He is to us, and what He wills that we should be to Him.

This is the true and profitable knowledge of God taught in every page of Holy Scripture, and necessary for all Christians. It cannot be too deeply studied, and without it none can become holy, for the substance of it is indispensably necessary to salvation. This should be the great object of our reflection and meditation, and of our constant prayer for light. Let no one fancy that he can ever know enough, or enter sufficiently into so rich a subject. It is in every sense inexhaustible. The more we discover in it, the more we see there is yet to be discovered. It is an ever-deepening ocean for the navigator, an unattainable mountain height for the traveller, whose scope of vision increases with every upward step. The knowledge of God grows in us together with our own holiness: both are capable of extending continually, and we must set no bounds to either.

Now this knowledge is not merely intellectual knowledge: it goes straight to the heart. It touches it, penetrates it, reforms and ennobles it, enkindling it with a love for all the virtues. Anyone who really knows God cannot fail to possess a lively faith, a firm hope, an ardent love, filial fear, a complete trust in Him in times of trial, and an entire submission to His holy will. He fears no difficulty in avoiding evil, nor in doing good. He complains of no rigour in God's law, but wonders at its mildness, and loves and embraces it in all its fulness. To the precepts he adds the counsels. He contemns earthly things, deeming them unworthy of his attention. He uses the things of this world as though he used them not. [2] He looks not at the things that are seen and are temporal, but presses forward towards those that are eternal. [3] The pleasures of this world do not tempt him, nor its dangers imperil him; neither do its terrors alarm him. His body is on earth, but his soul, in thought and desire, is already in heaven.

It is from the sacred Scriptures, rightly studied, that such knowledge is drawn, but many read them without understanding them, or understand them only according to the letter and not the spirit. The sacred writings are the principal source of all that God has pleased to reveal to us of His essence and perfections, His natural and supernatural works, His designs regarding man, the end He wills him to attain, and the means conducive to that end. Therein we see that God is the beginning of all things; that He governs all and intends all for His glory, and has accomplished all things for Himself, there being no other end possible for Him. We see the plan, the economy and sequence of religion, and the intimate connection of the rise and fall of empires with that supreme end. In a word, all that man needs to know concerning his salvation and that can fill his soul with fear, veneration and the love of God, is to be found in the tradition of the Church and Holy Writ, and there alone.

True, this knowledge is to be found in the writings of the saints also, and in other pious works. These are, however, but a development of what is contained in tradition and Scripture, and are good in the measure in which they express their meaning more clearly, and explain them more fully.

But, above all, this knowledge is to be found in immediate intercourse with God by prayer and meditation. Come ye to Him and be enlightened, sayst he Psalmist. [4] God is Light, and in Him there is no darkness whatever. His presence casts out darkness in him who prays. Indeed, the soul comes away from prayer better instructed concerning divine things, than learned men are by all their study. Many a simple and unlettered soul, taught in the school of divine Love, speaks of God more fittingly and nobly, more fluently and fervently, than the ablest doctors who, unless they are men of prayer, speak and write of heavenly things in a dry and uninspiring manner, devoid of grandeur, warmth and fervour.

But besides this knowledge, which may be called illuminative since it appertains to the mind, there is another kind of knowledge which consists in sensitiveness and is the portion of the heart. This is sweeter, stronger and deeper. It is a kind of experimental knowledge given by

God of Himself and of His presence. He seems to say to the soul: O taste and see that the Lord is sweet. [5] The advantage of this knowledge beyond the other is that it binds the will to Godmuch more strongly. Here the soul no longer acts of itself; it is God Who acts in it, and sets it aglow with a spark of His own bliss.

St. Antony knew God after this manner, when he complained that the sun rose too early and put an end to his prayer. So did St. Francis of Assisi, when he spent whole nights repeating with wonderful gladness the words: My God and my All. This sense of God, this experimental knowledge, has been the desire of all the saints, and the fruit of their union with Him. But if God is to give Himself thus to us, we must give ourselves wholly to Him; for, as a rule, He bestows this great grace on none but His best beloved. When, like St. Francis, we have given up all things; when God becomes for us, as for him, our sole good, then we may as truly and as earnestly say: My God and my All.

To explain this experimental knowledge of God is impossible. What is solely the heart's concern presents no idea to the mind, and is not to be expressed in words. How can we expect words to express supernatural things, when they are inadequate to represent mere natural affections and feelings? But for one who has not experienced them to call such things dreams and fancies, is the same as to deny the effect of natural love on the heart, because one has not experienced it. What is certain is that this sense of God elevates the soul to a greater height than any illuminative knowledge can do, and renders it capable of heroic designs and of the greatest sacrifices.

The knowledge of ourselves is no less precious and no less necessary to sanctity than the knowledge of God. To know ourselves is to render ourselves justice. It is to know ourselves exactly as we are; to see ourselves as God sees us. What does God see in us? Sin and nothingness: no more. That is all we can call ours; all the rest comes from God, and must be attributed to Him. When we know ourselves thus, what must be our humility, our contempt and hatred of self?

I am absolutely nothing. From all eternity, I was not, and there was no reason why I should exist, nor why I should be what I am. My existence is the simple effect of God's will: He bestowed it on me as it pleased Him, and it is He Who keeps me in being. Were He to withdraw His all-powerful hand for one instant, I would fall back into nothingness. My soul and body and the good qualities of both, everything that is estimable or pleasing in me, comes from God. On that foundation my education has done its work, and, seen in its proper light, that very education is more the gift of God than the fruit of my own industry or application.

Not only what I am, but what I possess, what I enjoy, all that surrounds me, whatever I meet with wherever I go--all comes from God, and is for my use. I am nothing; and, apart from God, all else is nothing. What, then, is there to love and esteem in myself or in others? Nothing but what God has freely given. Whence it follows that in all that is of itself nothing, and exists only by the will of God, I must only love and esteem God and His gifts. And this is a strong foundation for humility and the contempt of self and created things.

But this is not all. I am sin, by my own will, by the abuse of my most excellent gift of liberty. When I say 'I am sin', what do these words mean? In the first place, they mean that in the depths of my nature, and even by my having been brought out of nothingness, I have the unhappy power of offending God, of becoming His enemy, of transgressing His law, of failing in my most essential duties, and of falling short for ever of my true end. And this power is so inherent in me as a creature that nothing can separate me from it. Since the Fall, the power of sinning has become a tendency, a strong inclination, to sin. Through Adam's fault, I lack the perfect equilibrium of liberty in which I would otherwise have been created.

In the second place. After having arrived at the age of reason, I have actually sinned and have been guilty of a great number of offences more or less grievous. There are very few, indeed, who have retained their baptismal innocence. As for venial sins, which are always serious, the greatest of saints --Our Lady excepted-- have not been exempt from them.

Thirdly, there is no sin, however great, that I am not capable of committing, if I am not always on my guard, and if God does not preserve me from it. It needs only an opportunity, a temptation, an act of unfaithfulness, to induce the most fearful train of consequences. The greatest saints believed this of themselves, and we would do well to have the same holy fear.

Then, having fallen, I am absolutely incapable of rising up again by my own strength, or of truly repenting of my sin. If God does not open my eyes and move my will, and extend to me a helping hand, all is over with me. I shall add sin to sin, shun amendment, and harden my heart and die impenitent, a frightful evil which I must always fear, no matter to what degree of virtue I have attained.

But still this is not all. To my wretched inclination to evil is added an equal distaste for what is good. All law is irksome to me and would seem to threaten my liberty. Every duty is unpleasant, every virtuous act costs an effort. Besides, in myself, I am incapable of any supernatural act, even of thinking of or planning any. I am in constant need of special grace, to inspire good actions and to help me in carrying them out.

In such a state, which is that of my whole life, how can I think well of myself? Of what can I boast? Is there anything of which I have not reason to be ashamed and confounded?

This is the self-knowledge imparted by faith, and borne witness to by my own feelings and experience. The purest and sanest of philosophers would never have taught me half as much. Man has ever been the chief object of the study and consideration of philosophers; but the most eminent genius, with all its penetration and researches, has never been able to arrive at a real knowledge of self. That, to my mind, is a most humiliating thing. If faith does not enlighten me, it is greatly to be feared that reason alone will never tell me that I came from nothing, and that God is my Creator. It is very doubtful if it ever told any of the ancient philosophers that truth. They were all ignorant, it would seem, of this primary relationship between man and God, which is the foundation of all the rest. And how strangely at a loss they were in consequence of their ignorance regarding the origin of man. What curious absurdities they uttered on the subject. And our modern unbelievers, refusing the light of revelation, have not fared much better.

As concerns our tendency to evil and repugnance for good, the inherent frailty of creatures, the nature of sin considered with regard to God, and the necessity of grace, the most religious philosophies had only a faint glimmering on some points and clear notions on none. Generally speaking, they were involved in complete darkness. (333) What did they know about the matter, then? What no one can be ignorant of: namely the miseries of life, the weakness of childhood, the infirmity of age, the natural defects of mind and body, the passions and their tyranny and disorder, the inevitableness of death but without any certainty of a future state. This was a wretched, miserable sort of knowledge, and made most philosophers bitterly revile nature, and accuse her of treating man like an unjust and unnatural stepmother. For the little they knew, they were right, of course, and the destiny of man must have appeared to them the more deplorable, since they could find no remedy for their troubles, either in their own vain systems or in the false religion of the people.

Yet they were offended rather than humbled by this knowledge, distressing as it was, because it was, in reality, too imperfect. For while unable to fathom the depth of our misery, it offered nothing to counterbalance the little it was able to perceive.

It is otherwise with our own holy faith. Whilst making man little in his own eyes, deeply humbling him and reducing him to a state of nothingness, and even of less than nothingness, at the same time it supports and comforts him and gives him hope; showing him what great reason he has to trust in God. More, it inspires him with a noble idea of himself, since it reveals to him his true greatness, the nobility of his faculties, his closeness to God, the sublimity of his destiny, the fatherly care of Divine Providence, the inestimable grace of redemption, and the price paid for his soul by the incarnate God. It also teaches him to respect his body as the temple of God, destined to share one day, by a glorious resurrection, in the soul's eternal happiness.

This is the knowledge that religion gives us concerning our human nature, and this light is sure, for it derives from an abiding revelation. It is bright and penetrating, and is constantly increased by the study and practice of the faith. It crushes our human pride, when we think of what we are in ourselves, and elevates the soul when we contemplate God's plans in our regard.

But in addition to the motives for humility furnished by the study of the Gospels and the practice of the moral law, God has other ways of deeply humbling those whom He destines for a high degree of sanctity. He makes them feel that their light is darkness, and their will weakness; that their firmest resolutions count for nothing, and that they are incapable themselves of meritoriously correcting the smallest fault, or of performing the tiniest act of supernatural virtue. He allows them to feel the greatest repugnance for their duties; their pious exercises are painful and almost intolerable because of the dryness, listlessness and weariness with which they are assailed. The passions they fancied dead come to life again and cause them strange conflicts. The devil tempts them in countless ways, and they seem abandoned to the wickedness and corruption of their own hearts, so that they see in themselves nothing but sin and a violent inclination to sin.

In the light of His infinite holiness, God shows them the impurity of their motives and the selfishness of their aims, the stain of self-love on their good actions, and its poison in their virtues. He reproaches them with their negligences and cowardice, with their faithlessness and self-seeking, with the desire for approbation and human respect. He brings them to hate and despise themselves for their ungrateful abuse of His many graces.

For their yet greater self-abasement, He appears to turn His face from them, and deprives them of all sensible gifts and graces, leaving them in miserable nakedness, from the sight of which they shrink, yet to which they cannot close their eyes. He seems to be angry with them and to forsake them. On the other hand, He allows men to suspect their piety and call it hypocrisy, to disturb them with calumny and persecution. And this, not only on the part of wicked men and ordinary Christians, but also on the part of persons of good understanding and exemplary life who, whilst decrying and ill-treating these servants of God, fancy that they are honouring their Master. Our Lord Himself, the Saint of saints, willed to bear all these miseries and contumely, and greater yet than these, because He made Himself the Victim for sin. And upon His own beloved friends He bestows a precious draught from the same bitter cup. Thus, perfecting them in humility, He perfects them in sanctity, making them proof against all temptations.

Let us ascend, then, and descend by this wonderful ladder of the knowledge of God and the knowledge of ourselves. With the help of grace, ascend as high as you can, and descend as low as you can; and, when you have done all in your power, ask our divine Lord to use all the means, known only to Himself, to raise you and lower you still further.

Strange paradox! The more we ascend, the less are we conscious of ascending; and the more we descend, the less we feel like having done so. Yet it is true. The more one advances in the knowledge of God, the more inadequate will our concepts of what He is and what He merits appear to be. So, too, the deeper we penetrate in our knowledge of ourselves, the more convinced are we that we do not despise or hate ourselves enough. Only thus shall we become both exalted and humble, and all unconsciously sanctified.

1.   Cf, Ps. xli. 8: Abyssus abyssum invocat... Deep calleth on deep
2.   Cf. I Cor. vii. 31
3.   Cf. Sic transeamus per bona temporalia, ut non amittamus
aeterna: Collect for third Sunday after Pentecost
4.   Ps. xxxiii. 6.
5.   Ps. xxxiii. 9.

Second Maxim: Christian liberty and the active and passive
ways

Yield your liberty to God, and have no will but His.

In order the better to comprehend what I have now to say, it
would be as well in the first place to establish certain
principles, on which all will, I think, agree.

When we were created God bestowed on us reason and
understanding in order that we might know and love Him.
It was His mind that we should enjoy this knowledge and
love eternally, and that such enjoyment should be our
reward; accordingly, we must merit that reward. And so
God placed us on earth for a certain space of time, known
only to Himself, and gifted us with liberty, that is, with
command over our actions so that, being performed by our
own will, they might merit praise or blame, reward or
punishment. Merit, praise and reward are thus attached to
the free fulfilment of the duties imposed upon us by God;
and blame and punishment follow the wilful violation of
those duties.

Liberty, in the abstract, has no essential power of doing
good or evil; otherwise God, Who possesses supreme
liberty, would not be free, because He can never will, or do,
evil. Therefore, our power of doing wrong does not proceed
from our liberty, but from two other causes.

The first of these is that, being necessarily dependent upon
God by a moral dependence, our actions should follow the
rule of His will, so that they are morally good if they
conform to that rule and morally bad if they do not. The
second is that, being defective in our very nature, we are
always liable to deviate from this rule. From these two

causes, combined with the free will which makes us masters of our actions, arises that fatal power of sinning, which it would be unjust and blasphemous to reproach God for having given us. It did, indeed, depend upon Him to prevent its effect, but no reason obliged Him to do so, and His supreme wisdom deemed it fitter to permit that consequence, since it could not be prejudicial to His glory.

Unquestionably, the most perfect liberty is that possessed by God, Who can only will what is good. Therefore, the more our liberty resembles His, the nearer it approaches perfection; whilst the more unlike it is, the more imperfect it becomes. The will to sin is thus a defect and an abuse of liberty, and the stronger and more habitual it is, the greater will be the defect.

It is obvious that we ought to desire never to abuse our liberty, but by our love of good and hatred of evil bring it into the closest resemblance to God's will. The more we are morally necessitated to good, the more shall we be free like God, Who is necessarily so by nature. And the more we are morally necessitated to evil, the more will our liberty be fettered. That is why St. Paul says that when the will yields to evil, it becomes the servant of sin; but being freed from sin becomes the servant of justice: [6] a two-fold servitude, of which the first degrades liberty, whilst the second exalts and perfects it.

For God Himself, if one may say so, is the servant of justice, and that infinitely more than we can ever be; and it is in this servitude that His perfect liberty consists. And if the word 'servitude' seems extravagant when applied to God, it is because He is Himself His rule, and can know no other rule than His own will. The words the apostle used, Our Lord had already used when He said to the Jews:

Whosoever committeth sin is the servant of sin; but He added: if the Son of man shall make you free, you shall be free indeed. [7]

Now grace alone can deliver us from the bondage of sin, and assure us true liberty. Whence it follows that the more our wills are subject to grace, and the more they endeavour to depend fully and constantly upon it, the freer they will become. Our perfect deliverance is reserved for heaven, where we shall once and for all be established in grace. But in this world, however completely we may have submitted ourselves to the dominion of grace, we are always liable to throw off the yoke, and must be always on our guard against this peril.

This peril will be more or less imminent, according as the soul continues to be its own master, or gives itself up freely to be dealt with as God wills. And so, all it has to do is to place itself in His hands, using its activity only in order to become more dependent on Him, allowing grace to act in its regard freely and fully in all circumstances, reserving no power to itself save to correspond with entire fidelity to grace.

These principles conceded, it is clear that the surrender of our liberty is the same thing as true devotion to God; because devotion, or devotedness, is only another word for forsaking our own will for the will of God. This gift of our liberty is made in two ways, one of which stresses what therein depends on ourselves, the other what depends upon God. It depends on ourselves to retain the exercise of our liberty, but to be determined that it shall be subject to the inspirations of grace, and to hold bravely to this resolution. It depends upon God to make Himself master of our liberty, once we have made it over to Him, governing it Himself directly, yet without doing violence to it, holding it captive in His hand. Hence the two ways of serving God, of which the one is called active and the other passive. Both are good; both are agreeable to God; both are interior and lead to sanctity.

Following the first way, the Christian makes due use of the faculties God has bestowed upon him, his memory, his understanding and will: these he exercises himself. Although acting under the inspiration of grace and fully determined to follow its direction, yet he preserves his liberty; deliberating, judging, choosing and determining his choice in all that pertains to his salvation. By meditation, he saturates himself with the truths of the Gospel; stirs his affection by acts of the will; applies these truths and draws conclusions from them as a guide to his conduct, and forms resolutions which he endeavours toput into practice; in general, putting to good use whatever the Holy Spirit may suggest to him in the way of personal devotion, or that he may find in the lives of the saints or in other spiritual works. Thus, by continual thought and perseverance, together with the aid of prayer, counsel and the use of the sacraments, he succeeds in correcting his faults and in acquiring the Christian virtues.

Most persons who have their salvation seriously at heart follow this way, which is the most common and that taught by most popular writers on the spiritual life. That is why we have so many methods, so many exercises and practices for learning to meditate, for hearing Mass, for confession and communion and so on. This is the usual way of beginning, and it must always be persevered in unless God Himself calls us from it. This point must never be lost sight of, and is of the greatest importance, as it destroys many illusions and saps the very roots of any kind of Quietism.

We enter the passive way when we feel ourselves drawn by the strong and sweet workings of grace which, in order to gain space for its action, as it were, leads us to suspend our own; when we are inwardly moved to yield up our heart and liberty and our natural self-government into God's hands, in order that He may govern them by His adorable will. Then God takes possession of the powers of the soul, acting upon them, and making them act according to His designs. Man only follows, though always freely, in the path marked out for him. He holds himself prepared to do at any moment what God requires of him. And God, by a secret inspiration, makes known to him what He requires; yet this inspiration never involves disobedience to the Church, to her rules, or to all lawful authority. On the contrary, there are no souls more docile or more submissive than those who walk in this way.

Here, then, all exercise of natural liberty with regard to interior things (for of such only am I speaking) consists in seconding--never in forestalling--the movements of grace. As soon as these movements are forestalled or resisted, the human spirit is plainly at work. In the state of which I am speaking, the Christian lies under the hand of God like an instrument on which and by means of which He works: not, however, a purely passive instrument but one which consents and cooperates by its own act, often with extreme repugnance, and with violence to itself. Its state may well be compared to that of a child writing under its master's guiding hand.

Now it is easy to see why this way is called passive, and wherein it differs from the active way. In the latter, the powers of the soul, aided always by grace, act, as it were, of themselves and by their own effort. It is like a child, writing from his master's copy, under his inspection and obedient to his teaching. We choose our subject for meditation, apply our mind to it, form our reasonings, make acts of love, and by the ordinary methods arrive at our conclusions. All this, as is obvious, is active.

The passive way is not without its action, but it is God's action which motivates ours. The soul remains freely attentive, pliant and docile under the divine inspiration, just as the child places his hand in that of his master, intending to follow all its movements. But just as the child, though able to write, waits until the master shall guide his hand, so the powers of the soul, held and suspended, only exert themselves on the object to which God applies them, and to the extent to which He applies them. This work is thus more simple and hidden, and for that reason less apparent, so that the soul often thinks that it is doing nothing, when the very opposite is the case.

The soul is naturally active and restless, but when subdued by the divine action which invites it to be still, dwells in habitual calm. In prayer, no distinct object presents itself to the mind, and as a rule it perceives things in an obscure and indistinct manner. The sense of God's presence is a peaceful and abiding feeling, which does not take the form of expressed affections. The heart is satisfied, but without any effort on its part. St. Teresa, and later St. Francis of Sales, used the comparison of a child at its mother's breast. When the soul is in the passive state, the lips speak and the hand writes of divine things, without premeditation. God Himself provides all that is necessary, and the very memory of it passes away. There is no studying to root out one's faults, or to acquire virtues by different means. By His continual action on the soul, by the practices He suggest, no less than by the interior trials with which He visits it, God insensibly purifies the soul of its faults, impressing on it the various virtues which He causes it to exercise on occasion, without so much as reflecting on them, or even knowing that it possesses them.

There is more of what is infused in the passive way, and more of what is acquired in the active. And yet what is infused is, in a manner, acquired also, because it costs something to preserve it and to cause it to grow.

Here I am only speaking of the ordinary passive way, otherwise called the way of pure faith. Of extraordinary states, rare in any case, in which are to be found ecstasies and so on, and in which the devil troubles body and mind alike with vexations and divers torments, I propose to say nothing, since they ought to be neither sought nor feared. Nor is it right to indulge in any kind of curiosity concerning these states, nor to read books about them, except when it is necessary to do so for the guidance of others.

Such in the main is the difference between the active and passive ways. All men can and ought to follow the first with the help of ordinary grace; only God can introduce us into the second. Yet it is not to be denied that many, through their own fault, either do not enter it, or fail to persevere in it. But it is also true that, in God's intention, the first should very often dispose souls to the second, if they responded more faithfully to grace, and were more generous, brave and simple; and if they could only make up their minds to get rid of their self-love, and the entrance were not barred by their many mistaken notions.

Now as this way is far more conducive to our sanctification, since it is God Who then undertakes it and works at it Himself, it is most important that we should put away all such mistaken notions, and neglect nothing that may open it to us, for I am persuaded that God calls more souls by that way than is generally supposed. The important thing is to recognize the signs of His invitation, and to follow them with docility.

Some persons are invited to it from their earliest years by an inward attraction, as we learn from the lives of many of the saints. If this attraction were followed, if good parents and instructors of youth, instead of discouraging it, would favour it and carefully put aside all that was adverse to it; if confessors would take pains to cultivate the first seeds of grace and to develop this germ of the interior life, the number of souls led by the Holy Spirit would be much greater, especially among women, who with their quiet education and natural disposition are more inclined to be led by this way. The innocence of childhood, when the soul is simple, tractable and unprejudiced, is unquestionably the most favourable to true devotion, and if children were early guided in that direction, by lessons suited to their age, and with the necessary tact, skill and patience, wonderful results would follow.

Others, later in life, after following for a long or shorter time the common way, find that they can no longer fix their minds in meditation, nor produce the same affections as hitherto. They even feel a kind of disgust for the methods they have so far followed. Something which they cannot explain leads them to suspend all action when at prayer -- it is God Himself Who is inducing them to it, by the peace and calm which He allows them to taste. When this state is not a temporary one, but persists in spite of repeated endeavours to return to one's former practice, it is an infallible sign that God wants to take possession of such souls and bring them into the passive way.

Others are prepared for it by distress, anxieties, temptations and set-backs, which they can neither understand nor explain. God, wanting to raise a new edifice in their hearts, demolishes the former one completely, destroying it to its very foundations. It is the work of an experienced confessor to discover God's designs in all this, and to encourage those who are in this painful state to make a generous sacrifice of themselves, and yield themselves without reserve once and for all to the divine will. The sacrifice made, all agitation ceases, and the soul experiences a peace hitherto unknown, and enters into a new world.

There are some persons who, though leading pious lives, are dissatisfied with themselves and with their state. They feel that God is calling them to something else, without, however, being able to express what it is they are looking for. An opportunity furnished by Divine Providence at last leads them to someone who, though unacquainted with them, and without very well knowing why, speaks to them immediately of the interior life. At once, their uneasiness ceases, and they are calmed and satisfied, and when least expecting it find what they have sought so long.

Not only good men but sinners, and great sinners too, are called by God to the passive way. Some, at the moment of their conversion, are suddenly transformed by grace, and become new creatures, like St. Mary Magdalen, St. Paul, St. Mary the Egyptian and St. Augustine. Others, after spending many years in exercises of penitence, are gradually raised to a state of sublime contemplation. It is difficult to believe, but it is nevertheless true, that the sudden and wonderful change wrought by divine mercy in sinners, is usually more perfect and solid than that wrought in the just. Full of a sense of their own wretchedness and of

God's overwhelming goodness, they give themselves to
Him more generously, are more deeply humbled by His
favours, and bear His purifying trials more bravely.

But all, whether just men or sinners, who have walked in
the passive way, have entered it in no other manner than by
giving up their liberty to God, entirely and absolutely,
saying with St. Paul: Lord, what wilt Thou have me to do?
[8] ... 'I am no longer mine but Thine'. They could not enter
it in any other way, for God only takes what is offered Him.
The violence He does to the soul at such times is always
very gentle, and He awaits the consent of the heart whereof
He would be the Master.

And what reason is there for fear in thus yielding ourselves
to God? His tender invitations, His earnest solicitations,
have no other object than our good, our true good, which
He understands infinitely better than we do, and which He
desires more keenly and alone can procure. Is not our
salvation incomparably safer in His hands than in our own?
If we trust Him unreservedly with our dearest interests, do
we not preserve them from all those dangers to which the
devil and our own hearts would expose them? Is any power
strong enough to wrest our souls from God, once He has
accepted them, unless we ourselves are cowardly and
faithless enough to draw back? Can we more strongly
induce God to take care of us than by surrendering
ourselves to Him?

And in reality, what can we do in the matter of our
salvation apart from what God enables us to do? Whom
have we to fear or mistrust most, God or ourselves? Surely,
our liberty is the means to our eternal happiness or loss.
But so long as we cling to the use of our free will, we run
the risk of misusing it: a risk which entirely disappears

when we commit our liberty to God, asking Him to hold it captive by the gracious chains of His grace. Are we afraid that He will use our liberty in spite of ourselves; and that what He desires of us He will not know how to urge us to desire too? And if we do desire it with all our hearts, how can we fear a Master Who will not ask anything of us but what we are most willing to give?

And what better use -- what more glorious for Him and more conformable to the eternal ideas His love has for us -- can we make of our liberty than to become His willing servants, placing ourselves under His yoke, and inviting Him to exercise in our regard all the plenitude of the power which belongs to Him by right? What heroic acts of homage, faith, love, trust and abandonment are not combined in this one sacrifice? And, given that God will continue to the end the work He has begun; that the victim having once offered himself as a holocaust to the good pleasure of God will allow himself to be uncomplainingly immolated, what purpose can that immolation have other than to procure the greatest glory for God and at the same time assure our own eternal reward? And to give to God our liberty, what is it but to do in this life what the blessed do in heaven?

There is no doubt that our self-love rebels with all its strength against such a sacrifice. It shudders at the mere idea of abandoning itself without reserve to God. What! Never shall I be able to dispose of myself again in anything; never be master of a single thought, a single glance, a single word. Submit to being led by the obscure paths of faith, by ways beset with danger, knowing not where to place my feet, and believing all along that I am being led to certain death! Consent to face the most delicate and dangerous temptations, to submit to rough trials and suffer terrible loneliness on God's part; and, on the part of men, violent contradictions, calumnies, humiliations, persecutions! In a word, lay myself down on the cross, permit myself to be bound to it, and suffer its pains until I draw my last breath! For such can be the result of the gift of one's liberty to God: such the meaning of the gift of self. And whether one actually has to suffer these things or not, one must be prepared for them, since the devotion I speak of knows of no exceptions.

Self-love revolts against the mere thought of these things. But what is self-love? A love blind, and no true friend of ours; the unhappy fruit of sin, an enemy of God and of our own happiness, that the Gospel bids us fight and pursue to the bitter end; that closes heaven's gate to us until it is utterly vanquished, and of which the soul must be completely purified, either here or hereafter in Purgatory, before we can enjoy the possession of God.

That being the case, it would seem that the more self-love opposes this sacrifice, the more reason have we to endure it. For not only does our self-love not know its true interests, but it is absolutely hostile to them. We need not be surprised, therefore, that it should set itself up against what threatens it with complete annihilation. Since the love of God and the love of self dispute the possession of our heart (which must belong to one or the other), ought we not to seize with joy the surest means of delivering ourselves from this dread enemy, since it is God Himself Who is undertaking to do that for us? Is it not better to be consumed in this world by the fires of charity, with the incomparable glory that it gives to God and untold merit for ourselves, than to be consumed by the divine justice in Purgatory, where God will receive glory from our loving sufferings, but without any increase of merit on our part?

Suffering for suffering, which is the greater? In this life, it is less a matter of justice than of real mercy; in Purgatory, it is rather inexorable justice, which must be completely satisfied. Here, our miseries do have their intervals of rest and consolation; there, nothing relieves the suffering, and there is no rest. Here, grace sustains us on the cross, and infuses a sweet unction unknown in Purgatory. If we have any faith, therefore; if we have one spark of love for God or any true love for ourselves, in whatever light we consider the matter, how can we hesitate in our choice?

I say, if we have any true love for ourselves. For what is such love? It is the desire and endeavour to obtain our most perfect well-being: in other words, it is the love of God and His glory, and the love of His interests, with which our own are so closely bound. There is no doubt that we shall love ourselves in heaven: but how? With the same love with which we shall love God; we shall be unable to have any other love than that. Could we form a separate act of love for ourselves, we should at once forfeit our beatitude.

Let us, then, even in this life, commence to love ourselves thus, by giving ourselves to God in order to love Him alone. This love, which will consummate our happiness in heaven, will give us even now a foretaste of that happiness. I would add one last consideration: it is that should we die, having made this generous act of consecration, God will take it as though we had passed a long life in the continual exercise of this devotion, since the will to do so was ours, though the execution of it was not in our power.

It may be objected that the passive way is not open to any and every person who would like to walk in it; and that, according to our own showing, no one can enter it unless God calls them. All this is true: but I say that there are certain states of mind which prepare us for such a call, and that these are within our power. And I say further: even if this call should never come, we shall have had the merit of preparing ourselves for it.

The first of these dispositions is to conceive a real desire (but always quiet and patient) to live under the influence of grace, and to offer ourselves repeatedly to God, in order that He may be pleased to reign in our hearts. The second is to perform all our good works with a view to obtaining this grace. And, finally, to be extremely faithful in all our relationships with God, corresponding with all His inspirations according to our present state. With that intention, we could not do better than make our own the prayer of that great saint who was so devoted to the greater glory of God:4444 Receive, O Lord, all my liberty. Accept my memory, my understanding and my whole will. All that I have and possess, Thou hast given me: to Thee do I restore it all, and deliver it up wholly to Thee that Thou mayest dispose of it. Grant me only Thy love and Thy grace, and I am rich enough: nor do I seek aught beside. [9]

6.   Cf. Rom. vi. 17, 18
7.   John viii. 34, 36.
8.   Acts ix. 6
9.   Prayer of St. Ignatius, in the 4th week of the Spiritual Exercises

Third Maxim: Good direction

Pray for a wise guide whom, when you have found, trust, revere and obey.

THE main reason which should lead a Christian to give himself to God is that He is the chief and, strictly speaking, the only director of souls. Christ is not only the Way, which He reveals to us by His doctrine and example, He is also the inward Guide, the Shepherd Who provides good pasture and, by secret inspirations and suggestions, leads His sheep to find it. Nevertheless, according to the order of His providence, He makes use of the ministry of priests for the direction of souls. To that ministry He attaches His grace, and through it He gives needful advice and instruction. He is the inner Master; He and He alone can speak to the heart. But He speaks to it most certainly when His ministers in the exercise of their functions speak to the outward ear. He wills that they be heard and obeyed, as His representatives.

Since, therefore, priests are the principal and usual means that God uses for the direction of souls and by them introduces us to the way of perfection, whoever aspires to that perfection (and all ought to do so according to their state) should, if they are free to choose, ask God to enlighten them in their choice in order that they may be rightly guided. Their prayer will surely be granted, if they ask with real faith.

In no matter, however, should one be more on one's guard against being influenced in one's choice by human motives, or by human prudence. We must beware of listening to the suggestions of self- love or nature, which seek ever to be flattered and spared, or to inspirations which are clearly not from God, and which will inevitably lead to deceptions most difficult to retrieve. There is no point concerning which we are more easily blinded, or more apt to be prejudiced. We must place the matter in God's hands, simply and honestly, and resolve to take whoever He indicates, in spite of prejudice or aversion, or of any human feeling whatsoever. The same caution must be observed when it is a question of changing one's director. Such a change may be right and desirable in certain cases; as, for example, when the director is unskilled or careless, wanting in firmness or gentleness, unspiritual in his direction, or for any other reasons which would seem to make him unsuitable. Having thoroughly weighed the matter in God's presence, we must then act firmly but impartially, putting aside all irrelevant considerations.

And the choice is all the more difficult in that good directors are very rare, and the external signs by which we may recognize them most deceptive. St. Francis of Sales used to say that scarcely could one find one in a thousand, if that! No doubt, the expression is a little exaggerated, but none the less they are scarce. Just think of the combination of qualities which go to form a good director. He must be a man of an interior spirit, experienced in spiritual things, utterly dead to himself and intimately united to God; devoid of self-will, desiring neither to rule nor dominate those whom he guides. He must seek in nothing his own glory or interests but solely the glory and interests of the Master he represents. He must be susceptible of no attachment save that inspired by charity, exercising his ministry with perfect independence; above all method and system, infinitely pliable to the inspirations of grace, able to follow different approaches to meet the different needs of souls and God's designs in their regard. He must know when to give milk to the young, more solid food to those more advanced in virtue, adapting himself to each age and state of the spiritual life. He must be wise with divine wisdom, gentle without softness, compassionate without weakness, firm without rigidity, zealous without precipitation. With the apostle, he must be all things to all men, [10] condescending in a certain degree to human misery, prejudice and frailty; ready to exercise unfailing patience and equity of mind; reproving, consoling, urging, restraining, yielding or resisting, as circumstances require; sustaining, encouraging, humiliating, revealing the patient's progress or withholding the knowledge, according to the soul's need. In a word, he must be a man who, in directing souls, does nothing of himself but wholly seconds the work of grace, neither hurrying nor retarding it. He follows grace step by step, going as far, but no farther, than it leads. Are such men common today? Were they even in the time of St. Francis of Sales, when the interior life was more known and practised?

We cannot, therefore, ask God too earnestly to send us such a director, for it is one of the greatest graces He can give us, one which will be the source of many others. Rightly used it will surely lead us to perfection. Would it not be intolerably presumptuous to make such a choice ourselves, and would it not be most dangerous to look upon it in any but the highest light?

The foregoing applies specially to religious communities, who need nothing less than a saint to direct them, whether it is a question of inciting them to fervour or maintaining them in it. Generally speaking, it is as well for the whole community to have the same confessor, who can maintain the same spirit throughout; but for this, especially in the matter of regularity, union and charity, he will need all the qualities I have enumerated above.

I am well aware that not everybody can choose his own confessor, and that it often happens that those who decide the matter for us may not always carry out God's intention for us. There is no doubt that it is very unfortunate to fall, whether one knows it or not, into the hands of a director who has not all the requisite qualities. Nevertheless, even in this case, God supplies what is lacking in His minister; He takes upon Himself to lead us in His ways, and never will He fail us if we do not fail Him. It was thus He directed St. Paul and St. Mary the Egyptian in the desert, and thus He directs those in heathen lands who are deprived of almost all human help. So, in country places, where priests are perhaps less zealous, the Holy Spirit Himself will always guide holy souls, and teach them the secrets of the interior life.

However that may be, once we have reason to believe that we have found the director God intends for us, we must not fail to give him our complete confidence. When we feel that his words enlighten our darkness, disperse our doubts, awaken us from languor, warm our heart and lead us to serve God more worthily; when we feel by experience that such a man is the instrument of God, really following up the secret operations of grace; above all if he leads us in the way of recollection and prayer and interior mortification (for that is the touchstone of true direction), we must no longer hesitate to place ourselves entirely in his hands, hiding nothing from him, so that he may search out and develop what is hidden even from ourselves.

Generally speaking, God inspires us with the will to begin by making a general confession, so as to inform the priest, not only of our past faults, but of the graces we have received, the dangers from which we have been preserved, the secret attractions we have neglected or followed, and the vices and temptations to which we are most subject. By this means, he becomes acquainted with our whole life and character, the habitual dispositions of our soul, the various tentatives of grace, the obstacles we meet, and the precise point where we stand. He is thus better able to see what God expects from us, and how he is to cooperate with His designs.

We can never be too open with our director in all that concerns our interior life, and, through the whole of his direction, nothing should be kept back, whether as to the lights given us by God, the desires and aversions felt by nature, or the suggestions of the devil, whose artifices we shall never unravel unaided. Anything which secret pride or the temptation of the devil leads us to hide or disguise, is just the very thing we should mention; however humiliating, it must never be concealed. It is also necessary to be on our guard against suspicions or prejudices concerning our director, and the thousand and one imaginations that flit across our mind, or which the devil inserts there in order to lessen our confidence and trust. For this is the one thing he wants to do. As soon as he sees that a director is working hard for our spiritual advancement, he seldom fails to inspire us with feelings of distrust and repugnance. One cannot be too watchful on this point. Almost always, the danger arises from our allowing ourselves to be too critical of the direction given us. 'Why has he forbidden me to do this? Why does he treat me like this?' And so we argue with ourselves; we make judgments and indulge in feelings of resentment, and generally our confidence is undermined, our obedience weakened, and we think of the man instead of seeing God in him.

Here I may remark that one of the most certain signs of a disposition to the interior life is that candour and delightful openness which leads us to hide nothing, neither our defects, our faults or our motives from our director; never to make excuses, speaking plainly even though it means that we shall be humiliated and be thought less of. How rare, and yet how precious in God's sight, is this humble ingenuousness.

But it is not enough to be open with our confessor. We must receive his advice and decisions as reverently as if they came from the lips of Our Lord Himself. There must be no arguing with him, nor must we even mentally dispute whatever happens to be contrary to our own ideas. In all that touches our conscience, we must submit our way of thinking to his, believe the good or evil he tells us of ourselves, never justify what he condemns, nor by false humility condemn what he approves. We pretend that we have not made ourselves clear; that he does not understand us; that he does not see what passes within us, as well as we do. But these are poor excuses, by which we assume the right of private judgment. The confessor judges us better than we can judge ourselves. Let us hide nothing knowingly, then, from him, and be at peace.

Apart from the fact that we are blind in all that concerns ourselves, we know very well that God wills to lead us by the way of faith and obedience; and that we are acting in a manner directly contrary to His intention when we make ourselves not only our own judges but judges of those who are guiding us. The devil tries to ruin us, through presumption or despair, by representing us to ourselves as better or worse than we really are. These indocile and unsubmissive judgments are always dictated by self- love. They lead the conscience into error and its consequent blindness. They are the beginning of scruples, anxieties and all those miseries born of the imagination. They expose the soul to the most subtle snares of Satan, and to the most dangerous of illusions.

The spiritual life has its dangers, and great dangers too, if it is misunderstood. Erroneous ideas of it are not uncommon. This evil must inevitably befall anyone who professes to judge of the workings of God or of our enemy Satan, and to distinguish by his own lights as to what proceeds from nature or from grace. Therefore, when we have clearly and honestly manifested our internal state to our director, we must humbly and quietly submit to his decision. Should he be mistaken -- which could be the case, for he is not infallible -- no harm will accrue to us from his error. God will always bless submission and obedience, and hinder or repair the effects of the mistake. He has bound Himself to do so by His providence, because it is His will that we should see Him in the minister who takes His place. This principle is the sure foundation and only basis of all spiritual direction.

I allow that it requires great faith always to see God in a man, who, after all, is subject to error and not exempt from faults; and that it is no little sacrifice to give up our own ideas and convictions in the very matters which concern us most deeply. But without this sacrifice there can be no submission of judgment, and without such submission there is no real direction.

Finally, we must faithfully and without delay perform all that the director bids us do. If, through weakness or indolence, or for any other reason, we have failed to do so, we must tell him so. By this fidelity alone shall we advance. He will often prescribe things that are very painful to nature; practices which will humiliate us in the eyes of others; practices sometimes so apparently petty and insignificant, that our pride will disdain them; practices opposed to our minds, our tempers, our dearest inclinations. But if he has the spirit of God he must act thus, because the design of God, of which he is the interpreter, is precisely our death to self. We must be determined, therefore, to obey him in all things wherein we do not perceive manifest sin. And if we think it right to offer any remonstrance, it must always be subject to his decision.

It would be wrong to put before him such difficulties and impossibilities as are often imaginary, or the effect of strong prejudice or temptation. At any rate, after stating them simply, if he pays no attention to them, we must submit and resolve to obey. This will be easier than it seems, for nothing is impossible to grace and obedience. And if the victory over self calls for great efforts, it will be all the more glorious and meritorious. Virtues are the gift of God, and He almost always bestows them as a reward for some signal effort. Then what was formerly difficult becomes easy. Any number of proofs of this are to be seen in the lives of the saints.

10.   I Cor. ix. 22

Fourth Maxim: The practice of the presence of God

*Be always mindful of the God Who is present everywhere,
and Who dwells in the hearts of the just.*

No spiritual practice is more to be recommended than that
of the presence of God; none is more useful, none more
profitable for advancement in virtue.

It is indispensable. How is it possible to grow holy and
attain to union with God, if we do not habitually think of
His presence? It is most efficacious. With God always
before our eyes, how can we help but try to please Him in
all we do, and to avoid displeasing Him? It is most simple.
In its simplicity, it embraces all other means of
sanctification. God present within the soul, our duties
become clear to us from moment to moment. It is most
delectable. What can be dearer than the continual
remembrance of God, what sweeter to one who desires to
love Him and to be wholly His? Lastly, it is a practice
which the willing soul cannot find otherwise than easy.

God spoke to Abraham saying . Walk before Me, and be
thou perfect. [11] He mentioned that one point only,
because it contains all. David says of himself, that he set
God always before him. Why? For He is at my right hand,
that I be not moved. [12] Had he continued faithful to his
word, the sight of a woman would not have led him to
adultery, and from adultery to homicide. All saints, under
both the Old and the New Law, have held to this more than
to any other rule. Indeed, it is so well known that I need not
press it, nor need I dwell on its advantages, for they are
known to all, saint and sinner alike. I shall confine myself,
therefore, to two points: one, to explain well what is meant

by walking in the presence of God; the second, to indicate the means that will most avail us.

The presence of God may be considered under different aspects. God is necessarily present in all men, good and bad alike; in the souls of the lost as in those of the blessed; in all creatures animate and inanimate.

God is also present to all things by His providence. He sees all things, not only our actions but even our most secret thoughts. He sees the good, and approves and rewards it; He sees evil, and condemns and punishes it. He rules all, directs all, according to His eternal designs, and in spite of all obstacles makes all things work together for His glory. [13]

In the souls of the just God is present in a special manner: that is, by sanctifying grace. The heart of the just is His dwelling- place, says St. Gregory. This presence is a presence of good-will, of charity and of union. It is the source of our merits, making us children of God, pleasing in His sight, and worthy of possessing Him eternally hereafter. It is given to us in baptism, and restored by penance. It is habitual, and continues as long as we preserve the grace to which it is attached. Although no just man can answer for it within him (since no one knows whether he is worthy of love or hatred [14]), yet, when he has fulfilled the rules laid down for procuring it, he may reasonably believe that God has graciously bestowed it on him, and he must do all he can to retain it.

God is also present to the soul by actual grace, which enlightens the mind and attracts the will. This presence is not necessarily continuous for, although grace is always being offered to us, it does not always act, because its action presupposes certain dispositions on our part. This presence acts more or less on sinners, inspiring them with a sense of sin, and calling them to repent. Some are ceaselessly pursued by it; they cannot allow themselves a moment for thought without hearing the voice of God, bidding them turn from their evil ways. Much more does it act on the souls of the just, to turn them from evil, excite them to holiness, and sanctify all their works. It is more felt and more efficacious, according as our attention and fidelity are more or less perfect.

Lastly, there is a presence of God which consists of an habitual infused peace. This presence first makes itself known by its sweetness, which as St. Paul bears witness, surpasses all understanding. [15] Afterwards, it is only perceived, without being strongly felt, and finally, it is enjoyed, like health, without being noticed. God does not thus bless with His presence all the just, but mostly those of whom He takes special possession, and whom He desires to place in the passive state. Others generally only experience its transitory effects.

The different kinds of God's presence being thus explained, it is easy to understand what is meant by walking in the presence of God. It is not merely just thinking about God, as a philosopher might do when he meditates on divine things, without applying them to himself. It is rather thinking of God, as affecting our habits and conduct; it is a deduction from that thought of the moral consequences in so far as they imply a rule of life. Thus, in the practice of the presence of God, it is a straightforward and devout will which must direct the understanding, and the heart will always have the chief share.

It is a mistake to think that this practice consists of violent efforts to force the mind to be always thinking of God. That is not possible, even in the most perfect solitude and detachment from earthly things. How much less so, then, in the case of persons living in the world, distracted by the cares of life, by business and domestic worries, and by a crowd of similar things. Are such people to be excused from attempting this practice? They would be, if the presence of God meant banishing every thought from the mind. But this is not the case: no Christian is exempt from this exercise on account of the circumstances of his state; indeed, it is compatible with the busiest life.

He walks, then, in the presence of God who, when he is free to do so, systematically arranges his time so that he can recall the presence of God at different times of the day --by meditation, for instance, or prayer, by assisting at Mass and similar devotions, by visits to the Blessed Sacrament, vocal prayer and so on; who, as in the sight of God, employs his time usefully and well, avoiding idleness, and in general keeping a curb on his imagination.

He walks therein who, apart from his morning and evening prayers (which no Christian should omit), in a day filled by necessary occupations, offers his principal actions to God, thanking Him for the food He sends, recalling Him from time to time, and making frequent use of short ejaculatory prayers during the day.

He also walks therein who, like Job, takes heed to all his ways, watches over his thoughts and words and works, in order to say and do nothing to wound his conscience and displease God. This practice is no constraint for one who fears God, still less for one who loves Him, and it is thus that all good Christians should act. It is nothing but a faithful preservation of sanctifying grace and of God's favour, which is the primary duty of every Christian.

He walks therein more entirely who, like David, keeps the issues of his heart, in order always to hearken to what the Lord shall say to him, and to the secret warnings He may give him; who studies to correspond to every inspiration of the Holy Spirit, and to perform every action under the influence of grace. All interior persons follow this method, which is the most apt for leading them to perfection.

Lastly, he walks therein still more perfectly who, having been favoured with the infused peace of which I have spoken, diligently endeavours not to part with it, dwelling always, as it were, within his own heart, in order to realize it; carefully avoiding anything that might disturb it or cause him to lose it, and eagerly embracing all that will help to preserve and increase it. This peace, as I have said, is purely the gift of God. It does not depend on ourselves to obtain it, but having been given it, we must do all in our power to preserve

As to the means which facilitate the exercise of the presence of God, some are general and some are particular. The first thing is to remove all obstacles. Once these are out of the way, the presence of God becomes as familiar to us, as free and as easy, in a way, as the act of breathing. We must mortify, therefore, our desire to see, hear and know things which are useless and which do not concern us. We must avoid all curiosity, for curiosity draws us out of ourselves, as it were, into the things themselves. The practice of the presence of God, on the contrary, recalls the soul to dwell within itself. We must keep a strong hand on the natural restlessness which incites us to come and go, ever changing our place, our object, our occupation. This restlessness is really the effect of that uneasiness which overwhelms us when we look within ourselves, and fail to find God there. All this inordinate eagerness and vehemence in our desires must be brought under control.

The imagination must be curbed, until it becomes accustomed to be at rest. If, in spite of our efforts, it runs away with itself, it must be led back gently, and gradually weaned from what it feeds on, what affects it vividly and strongly, such as vain shows, exciting books, and a too great application to the imaginative arts. Nothing is more dangerous or more incompatible with the practice of the presence of God, than to give the imagination too free a rein. It is true that we are not wholly masters of that faculty, the wanderings of which are the torment of religious souls. This is a great humiliation, and a fertile source of scruples for those who are unable to despise them. But what is in our power is to refuse the imagination the objects it seeks with such avidity, and to which it clings with such tenacity. Avoid everything, therefore, that can serve it as pasture, which dissipates it, excites it, and calls for its too great indulgence. Keep, too, a great liberty of mind and heart, dwelling on neither the past nor the future. Remember that the present moment alone is at our disposal. Put aside all useless thoughts, for it is equally contrary to the presence of God to think too much or too little. Do not meddle with other people's affairs. Set your own in order, without undue anxiety as to the result; be reasonably careful over them, and leave the rest to God. Do not take too much upon yourself, but reserve some time for rest and recollection. It is quite right to render services to others, and to undertake works of mercy. But these things have their measure, and cease to be right when they do harm to the soul. So much for liberty of mind.

As to liberty of heart, let nothing enter therein which will affect it too sensibly, or agitate and disturb it, or excite excessive desire, fear, joy or grief: nothing, in fact, which is likely to captivate it or turn it aside from its one true object. As this exercise is one of love, the distraction of the heart is far more harmful to it than that of the mind. The more the mind and heart are free, the more shall we be disposed to remain in God's presence, for God is always the first object that offers itself to either, when they are emptied of all else.

The particular means to this end are the frequent use of such things as may remind us of God: as, for instance, the crucifix, religious prints or pictures, texts from the Scriptures or Fathers, the sign of the cross (as was the habit of the early Christians, who, according to Tertullian, were accustomed to begin all their actions by making that sign). The mind is drawn by the meaning behind these things, and nothing is more apt for steadying or recalling the imagination. It is good, also, to know by heart a certain number of aspirations drawn from the Psalms or from other parts of Scripture, and to use them often. After a little practice, these habits will become easy and pleasant. If daily meditation is practised, some thought or affection that appeals to one will be enough to nourish the soul during the day. It is for everyone to choose for himself the method that suits him best, and follow it or change it according to the benefit he receives.

But the best way of all to acquire the practice of the habitual presence of God is to meditate often on Our Lord Himself and on His mysteries, especially His Passion. The various representations of Our Lord's sufferings strike vividly the imagination; the mind finds in them endless matter for solid and holy reflection; the heart is touched and moved, and the feelings stirred which nourish devotion. I shall speak of this, however, at greater length, in the following chapter.

As for those are in the passive way, there is no need to teach them any particular method of remaining in the presence of God. The Holy Spirit will lead them to the use of all suitable methods, and they have only to submit themselves to His guidance. In the beginning, they will feel too much happiness in their secret intercourse with God ever to be tempted by anything that might interrupt it: even the thought of such a thing is repugnant to them. Later on, however, when God withdraws His sensible presence and drives them, so to say, out of themselves, so that they may not notice the work He is doing within them, they may seek in creatures the consolation they no longer find in God. This is fatal, for God punishes with jealous severity any unfaithfulness in this matter, and should they persist in their infidelity, they will inevitably lose all that they have gained. Without committing themselves, however, to any particular line of conduct, they must be very faithful to the inspirations of grace, omitting no accustomed practice voluntarily, but persevering in exterior and interior mortification, believing that as God had given more to them than to others, so He will require more at their hands.

The habit of the presence of God, like all other habits, is difficult to acquire, but once acquired, is easy and pleasant to preserve. The sweet thought of God, so nourishing to the soul and so essential at all stages of the spiritual life, makes all other thoughts intolerable and vain. As the soul progresses, it sees God more dearly in everything. The very sight of created things recalls the thought of their Creator, while the perfection of His works fills it with delight. In all that happens, whether in the world or in the Church, whether temporal or spiritual, great or small, adverse or prosperous, the faithful soul perceives its Lord, Who manifests Himself equally in all things. It sees itself only in God; its interests only in God's interests; its glory in His glory; its happiness in His happiness. The things of earth fade into the distance, and the soul becomes a stranger to them. Already it feels itself transported into heaven, and judges of everything as it will one day judge of them in eternity. Such are some of the admirable effects of the practice of the presence of God.

11. Gen xvii. 1
12. Ps. xv. 8
13. Cf. Rom. viii. 28.
14. Cf. Eccles. ix. 1

Fifth Maxim: Devotion to Our Lord

Keep close to Our Lord in His mysteries, and draw the purest love from His salutary wounds.

Christ is the centre, not only of our religion, but of our spiritual life. By whatever path the soul may be led, active, passive, ordinary or extraordinary, He is the one guide and pattern, the chief subject of its meditation and contemplation, the object of its affection, the goal of its course. He is its physician, shepherd, and king; He is its food and delight. And there is no other Name under heaven given to men, whereby they may be saved, [16] or come to perfection.

Therefore, it is both absurd and impious to imagine that there can be any prayer from which the humanity of Our Lord may or ought to be excluded, as an object not sufficiently sublime. Such an idea can be nothing but an illusion of the devil. Contemplate the perfections of God, if you are drawn to do so: lose yourself, if you will, in the Divine Essence; nothing is more licit or praiseworthy, provided grace gives wings to the flight and humility is the companion of that sublime contemplation. But never fancy that it is a lower course to look and gaze upon the Saviour, whenever He presents Himself to your mind. Such an error is the effect of a false spirituality and of a refined pride, and whether we are aware of it or not leads directly to disorders of the flesh, by which intellectual pride is almost invariably punished.

Know, then, that as long as the soul has free use of its faculties, whether in meditation or in simple contemplation, it is primarily to Our Lord that we must turn. Pure contemplation, in which the understanding alone is exercised upon an entirely spiritual subject, is too high for weak minds like ours, encumbered with a weight of flesh, and subjected in many ways to material things. For some, it is less a prayer than an intellectual speculation. With others, it is a matter of the imagination, in which they lose sight both of God and of themselves. Why, the very seraphim cover themselves with their wings in the presence of the Divine Majesty, and we would dare to raise our eyes and gaze thereon!

Besides, this contemplation is too bare and dry for the heart, which finds no nourishment therein. The abstract consideration of infinite perfection contains nothing to stimulate us to virtue, or sustain and encourage us when low. The repose obtained by this supposed prayer is a false one, and dangerously near to Quietism. It leaves the soul dry, cold, full of self-esteem, disdain for others, distaste and contempt for vocal prayer (which in our weakness we need), and for the common practices of piety, charity and humility, and indifferent even to the most august and holy of the sacraments.

If the powers of the soul are bound in time of prayer, then it is possible that we may not be able to think of Our Lord, or of any other subject. God, desiring to humble the mind, to subdue our natural activity and root out from our heart its immoderate love of sensible consolations, sometimes leaves the soul for years in a void, during which neither Our Lord nor any other distinct object is presented to it.

However, in the first place, this is not the act of the soul itself, but a sort of martyrdom in which it acquiesces because such is the will of God. And when, during this fearful nudity, Our Lord occasionally reveals Himself, with what joy does not the soul welcome Him and converse with Him, during the brief moments of His stay!

How happy when I find at last,
How joyous when I hold Him fast!

But equally, what anguish does not the soul experience, when it is plunged once more into the night of its own nothingness.

In the second place, the soul thus treated endeavours to make up during the day for the loss from which it suffers in time of prayer. It thirsts to be joined in Holy Communion to Him Who, in these seasons of dearth, is its only stay, its only food. It spends itself in holy ejaculations; it invents divers practices whereby to invoke and adore Him throughout the day in His various mysteries. It seeks Him in spiritual reading, visits Him in His holy House, turns to Him for grace, and has recourse to Him in temptation. There is no soul, really and truly interior, whether passive or not, but strives to live in Him and by Him and for Him, and to have for Him a deep and continuous love.

How could it be otherwise? God the Father gave Him to us for this very purpose. He became man in order to unite us with Himself. Sin had separated God and man too widely; Christ assumed our nature in order to repair that separation. No man cometh to the Father, but by Me, He said. [17] No man abideth in the Father, but by Him. To forget for one instant that sacred humanity would be to sever our sole link with the adorable Trinity. How can one conceive that the Father, Who draws us to His incarnate Son, could ever wish to see us in a state of prayer in which it would be an imperfection to think of that Son, or wherein it would be necessary to separate His humanity from His divinity, and

neglect the one in order to occupy oneself with the other.
The mere thought of such a thing would be both absurd and
blasphemous.

St. Paul was not only an interior man, but in the passive
state: bound, as he himself says, by the Holy Spirit, [18]
Who in a sovereign manner was the guide of all his
thoughts, his feelings, his words, and of all he wrote;
indeed, of the whole course of his apostolic work. Can one
doubt that he was in the passive way to an extraordinary
degree, in view of what he tells us of the greatness of his
revelations, the humiliating temptations to which he was
subject in order to keep him humble, and of the gifts of the
Holy Spirit which he possessed in such plenitude? [19] Yet
his epistles are full of Christ; he speaks of nothing else, and
with what transports of gratitude and love! The mere
mention of the divine Name is enough to send him into
such raptures that his words cannot contain his thoughts,
and pile up their images in the liveliest disorder and
embarrassment, in their endeavour to express the sublimity
of his supernatural enthusiasm. Again and again, he urges
the faithful to study Christ, to imitate Christ, to 'put on'
Christ, [20] to do all and suffer all in the name of Christ.
[21]

He invites the faithful to be followers of him as he is of
Christ. [22] He affirms that he fills up in his person what is
wanting in the sufferings of Christ; [23] that is, by his
labours and sufferings, he applies to himself the merits of
the Passion of his divine Master. He assures us that he
carries the marks of Jesus in his body; [24] and, finally, as
though unable to say more, he declares that he no longer
lives, but that Christ lives in him. [25]

And what am I to say of St. John, the beloved disciple who, as the eagle dares to gaze with open eyes upon the sun, contemplated the eternal generation of the Word in the bosom of the Father? Not only literally, as at the Last Supper, but continuously throughout his life, he leant upon the bosom of the Saviour. And who ever reached a higher state of contemplation, or led a more interior life? And what is his Gospel but the most sublime and touching exposition in its simplicity of Jesus in His divine nature, of all that He longs to be to us and wants us to be to Him; as well as of the most intimate desires of His Sacred Heart, both for the glory of the Father and the salvation of men? What are his epistles but a tender exhortation for all men to love Christ, and to love one another even as He has loved us? [26] What is the Apocalypse but a prophetic description of Christ, here below in His Church, and hereafter in the elect, washed and purified in His blood, [27] and of His temporal and eternal triumph over His enemies? The apostle was drawing near the end of his life and was consummated in the most perfect union with his Master, when the Holy Spirit dictated to him these divine words. Dare one, in view of this, say that there is a kind of prayer so high that the sacred Humanity has no place in it? With what horror would not St. John have received and rejected so detestable a proposition.

Among the saints, men and women, ancient and modern, were assuredly a great number of contemplatives, who followed either the active or passive way. But where will one find any to whom Christ and His mysteries were not at once the centre and foundation of their prayer; and who in their writings have not urged Our Lord as the unique Way that leads to perfection? There are none; there never have been, and there never will be.

You, then, who aspire to the interior life, that is to a life of genuine piety, enter, as the author of the Imitation counsels, into the hidden life of Jesus. Study to know Him well, to make His most intimate thoughts your thoughts. Let this knowledge be the constant subject of your prayers, your reading and meditation; refer everything to it as to its centre and term. You will never exhaust it: you will not even fathom its depths. The saints have ever discovered new treasures in the measure in which they advanced, and all have admitted that the little they knew was nothing to what they longed to know.

But it is not enough to study Christ: we must stir our hearts to love him, for the love of God and the love of God made man are one and the same thing. Let this love be the food of your soul; let it be the object of all your spiritual exercises, in order that you may grow in that love from day to day. If any man love not Our Lord Jesus Christ, says St. Paul, let him be anathema. [28] To love Him in a half-hearted manner is to be but a poor Christian. The true Christian longs and strives to love Him more and more, knowing that He can never be loved as He deserves to be loved, or in the measure of His love for us.

But to love Him without imitating Him would be both vain and sterile. Therefore, be imitators of Christ. He is our model, perfect in every detail: a model for all states and for all conditions. To all men, in every conceivable circumstance, Christ in His mysteries, His virtues and in His doctrine, gives us the examples and lessons He proposes for our imitation. His teaching furnishes us with the most powerful motives, whilst His grace and the sacraments provide us with the most efficacious means.

But above all, meditate on His Passion; cling to His Passion. Reproduce in your own life those virtues of which His Passion presents the most living picture.

Seek in your prayers to draw love from His salutary wounds, above all from His pierced Heart. Remember that His sacred Passion is the foundation of the whole of our faith: that He came on earth to die upon the Cross; that it was by this sacrifice He made satisfaction to the Father and expiation for our sins; opened heaven to us and merited all the graces that will bring us there. Remember that the sublime sacrifice of our altars, which is the central act of our faith, is but the memorial, the renewal and extension of the sacrifice of Calvary. Remember, too, that it was He Himself Who committed to priests and laity the duty to offer His Body and receive It as food, in memory of His crucified love for men.

The crucifix is, and always will be, the dearest book of devout souls. It speaks to the senses, to the mind and to the heart. No other language is so eloquent or so touching. It is within the understanding of the most simple and ignorant, yet is, at the same time, above the comprehension of the greatest intellect and the highest learning. It says all, teaches all, answers all. It provokes the greatest efforts, consoles and sustains in times of the most bitter sorrow, and changes the very bitterness into sweetness.

The crucifix invites sinners to do penance, causing them to realize all the malice and enormity of their crimes. It reproaches them with as much gentleness as force; offers them the remedy, assures them of pardon, and excites in their hearts feelings of contrition as loving as they are sincere. It encourages the just, making the way to virtue easy. It persuades them to renounce and fight their passions, rendering them deaf to the cries of self- love, which dreads poverty, suffering and the afflictions that mortify the mind and flesh. Above all, it humiliates and destroys human pride, the source of all vice and sin.

The crucifix draws us to a state of recollection and prayer, to the interior life. It speaks to us of gentleness, patience, pardon for injuries done to us, love for our enemies, charity towards our brethren, even to the offering of our lives for them. It provokes us to love God by revealing to us the extent of His love for us, and how truly He merits to be loved in return. It impels us to submission and to the perfect conformity of our will with the divine will, whatever the cost, and to confidence and abandonment in times of the greatest desolation. In a word, it engages us to the practice of virtue and the avoidance of vice, in a way so gentle and persuasive that it is impossible to refuse.

Devout soul, do you desire to attain to union with God, to receive the precious gift of His continual presence which makes all labour light? Then spend some time every day before the crucifix. Take no other subject for your meditation. Gaze at it, hold it in your hands, pray to Jesus hanging on the Cross, and ask Him to be your master and director. Bid your mind be silent in His presence; let your heart alone speak. Tenderly kiss His hands and feet, press your lips to the wound in His sacred side. Your soul will be moved, and torrents of grace will flow into it, and with joy you will draw waters out of the wells of salvation. [29] You will run in the way of the commandments, [30] for the Cross contains them all.

Say not that the sight of the crucifix does you no good; that it leaves your heart cold and insensible; that, however much you try to express your love, you have no words wherewith to do so. If you cannot speak, you can listen. Stay silently and humbly at your Saviour's feet. If you persevere, He will not fail to instruct, nourish and fortify you. And if you feel nothing of this at the time, you will perceive it in your conduct, in the gradual change in your disposition. We are impatient, and our senses cry out to be satisfied, and, for this reason, we abandon the most profitable practices just because they do not succeed immediately. Persevere, I say. You have greatly abused the love of Jesus, let Him now try yours a little. He will crown your perseverance with success, and the gift of prayer will be your reward.

Our Lord's Passion has always been the particular devotion of those saints who have been renowned for their hidden life. Such were St. Bernard, St. Francis of Assisi, St. John of the Cross, St. Catherine of Siena, St. Gertrude, St. Teresa and many others. And any numbers have written on the subject. Yet if these great mystics tell us that there are states in which one loses sight of Our Lord, they will always add that these experiences are the expression of stages in Christ's own life, and that it is He Who impresses on the soul His own dispositions as He grew from childhood to His death. Step by step Jesus leads us to pass through these various stages, commencing with sensible joys, and passing to exterior and inner sufferings both of body and soul; humiliations, contradictions, calumnies and persecutions on the part of others; temptations on the part of the devil, and trials and interior aridity on the part of God.

During these trials, we do not see that it is Our Lord Who is crucifying us, for that would be too great a consolation. For our own good, it is essential that we should be unaware of His part in all this, if we are to exercise our faith and trust and so reap the full benefit of our sacrifice. When Jesus thus hides Himself from us, we suffer more, it is true, but we merit more. And should we have to pass the whole of our life in darkness and aridity, our trust and obedience will grow all the stronger.

Thus we are never more truly and intimately united with Our Lord than when there seems to be a thick veil between Him and our soul, which we would like to lift but cannot. It is in this sense solely that we must understand all approved spiritual writers who have treated of this matter, and it would be a grave injustice to accuse them of any kind of Quietism.

What I have written regarding Our Lord applies also to Our Lady and the saints. All devotion to the saints has its source in the love of Christ, sole author of their sanctity, and always brings us back to Him, no matter at what degree of sanctity we have arrived. To want to do away with such devotion, even temporarily, under whatever pretext, would be gravely wrong.

And who would dream of suggesting that there is any way of prayer, in which we can afford to do without Mary; wherein the thought of her virtues and greatness would be a hindrance? Is it not through her that we approach the Son, even as it is through the Son that we go to the Father? Is she not most intimately connected with the three Persons of the most adorable Trinity? Do not all aspects of our faith lead us to be in touch with her? Is she not the channel of graces, and is not hers the most powerful mediation that one could employ with her Son?

If, then, in times of darkness, trouble and desolation, we are deprived of the consciousness of Mary's most powerful aid in time of prayer, it is for the same reason that we are deprived of the sense of Our Lord's own closeness. But just as it is then that Jesus, all unknown to us, draws ever closer to us, so it is then that He communicates to us a deeper and more tender love for His Mother. And in any case, the deprivation I speak of does not prevent us in our morning and evening prayers, and during the course of the day, addressing our devotions to Mary, and honouring her in various ways.

And so it is with the other saints, with whom as with the angels we ought to hold a holy commerce. We should always have the intention of honouring them and praying to them, whatever our state. Indeed, the higher our state, the greater our love for them will grow, although we may not always be free to think of them or invoke them. Yet, short of a special suspension of our faculties on God's part, I doubt if a day passes, when we are not able to pay them at least something of the devotion due to them.

15.   Phil. iv. 7
16.   Cf. Acts iv. 12
17.   John xiv
18.   Acts xx. 22
19.   1Cor. xii. 2 ff
20.   Rom. xiii. 14
21.   Col. iii. 17
22.   I Cor. iv. 17 and xi. 1
23.   Col. i. 24
24.   Gal. vi. 17
25.   Gal. ii. 20
26.   I John iv. 11

27.   Apoc i. 5
28.   I Cor. xvi. 22
29.   cf Isaias xii. 3.
30.   Cf. Ps. cxviii. 32

Sixth Maxim: The Sacraments of Penance and Holy
Eucharist

*Make good use of the two sacraments, whereof one brings
cleansing, and the other life.*

We all know that, after baptism which regenerates but can
only be supplied once, the two chief springs of grace are
the sacraments of Penance and the Holy Eucharist, which
may be renewed as often as the soul stands in need of them.
The former cleanses it from sin and renders it pure in God's
sight; the latter maintains its spiritual life by uniting it with
the very Author of that life. Therefore the right use of these
two sacraments greatly tends to sanctification, and his
salvation is assured who does his best to receive them
worthily, and profit by them fully.

It would lead me too far were I to treat of this matter at
length, and my subject does not require it of me. I am not
now writing for those who only go to confession and
communion in order to obey the precept of the Church.
This I will say, in case my book falls into their hands. As
long as they do only so much as is absolutely of obligation,
they run a great risk of not being rightly disposed for the
reception of these sacraments. If they have any bad habits,
it is most unlikely that they will overcome them, so long as
they go to confession and receive communion only once a
year, and their salvation, to say the least of it, will be
imperilled.

Nor am I writing for those who are accustomed to confess
and communicate only on the great festivals. It may well be
that their lives will be exempt from grave sins, but they are
surely wanting in zeal for their sanctification, and respond
neither to the desires of the Church nor to Our Lord's

intention in instituting these two sacraments. I would advise them to consult some good book on the advantages of frequent confession and communion; to obey the pressing invitation of the Church, and to listen humbly to the advice of their confessor.

I write only for those who, being resolved to lead a holy life and, knowing that frequent participation in the sacraments is one of the most effectual means to sanctification, have formed the good habit of going to confession and communion weekly and even oftener, as their occupations permit and their confessor recommends. I write also for those who have given themselves to God, such as priests and religious, who by their rule of life are encouraged to frequent confession and communion.

In addressing, therefore, such persons I must confine myself only to what is absolutely essential, if I am not to make this work too long. In any case, the general rules in regard to frequent confession and communion are sufficiently well known.

Now in the ancient Church, confession was much rarer, communion much more frequent. The bishop was then the only, or almost the only, confessor; and if the early Christians, who communicated whenever they assisted at the Holy Sacrifice (not to mention the times they communicated in their own homes), had gone to confession as often as devout folk do now, the bishop, it is obvious, would have had no time to hear them. As holy as their lives were, nevertheless some small faults escaped them daily, which they did not deem necessary to confess. If they had aught against their brethren, they sought reconciliation before offering their gifts; [31] and as for venial sins, they believed, as St. Augustine teaches, that these were wholly remitted by the recitation of the Lord's Prayer. They only applied to the bishop or to someone deputed by him, for sins of some little magnitude or concerning which they were in doubt; and we may well believe that their consciences were at least as delicate as those of devout persons of the present day.

As time wore on, and the number of confessors increased, the facility with which one could apply to them made confession much more frequent, whilst the holy custom of communicating whenever present at Mass being lost, the idea began to take root that it was necessary to receive the advice or permission of the confessor before going to communion, and this led to much more frequent and regular confessions; so much so, that people began to think that they had to go to confession always before communicating.

Now such continual confessions, when made a matter of routine or obligation, are subject to abuse. They give rise to anxiety and scruples. The penitent worries himself to find something to say. He dwells upon thoughts that had better be despised, and exposes himself to be wanting in contrition. Often there is no matter for absolution, and yet it would be distressing if the confessor gave none. The worst of it is that, without confession, such persons will not go to communion, when they could and should do. No one knows what it costs sensible confessors to bring such souls to reasonable practice in this matter. They take fright and are scandalized. Very often, nothing can be done with them, and the confessor is obliged to yield to their contumacy.

Another abuse, still greater and more common, is that of believing that all perfection consists in the frequent participation of the sacraments. Many think themselves saints because they communicate weekly or daily, who yet never dream of correcting their faults; who perhaps do not even know them, so blinded are they by self- love. They are impatient, harsh, censorious, full of self-esteem and contempt of their neighbour, proud of the multitude of their external observances, and without the slightest idea of interior mortification. All the profit they derive from their communions and other pious exercises consists in spiritual vanity, secret pride, and all the subtle vices engendered by devotion grafted on to self-love.

A third abuse is that of treating confession and communion as matters of routine. Those who fall into this error come to the sacraments without any, or with only superficial, examination of conscience. It may be that they are afraid of breaking their rule and of attracting attention; or their director may have given them certain orders. And so these most holy actions are performed as perfunctorily as if they were the most ordinary affairs.

Let us consider each sacrament separately. The thing most to be feared in the matter of frequent confession is that, either the examination of conscience is insufficient, or else it is exaggerated and scrupulous. Persons of a light or thoughtless nature, or whose devotion is cold and indifferent, are liable to the first fault. Some only consider their external acts, and scarcely give a thought to what passes within them. Others have their pet sins, of which they seem quite unconscious, or they go through a regular form of examination which they repeat by heart to the confessor, nearly always in the same order and in the same words. There are others also who, being habitually subject to venial sins, such as breaking certain rules, and with no idea of correcting themselves, presume to leave them out of their examination and confession altogether. In general, their examination is badly done, either from ignorance or for want of watchfulness in the intervals between their confessions, or because they are not sincere in their desire for perfection.

On the other hand, very timid souls, who have lively imaginations or are narrow-minded, are apt to examine themselves too severely or too anxiously. They see faults in everything, and these faults, which are often nothing at all, they exaggerate and turn into immense affairs. They confuse thought with consent, first involuntary movements with determined acts . They worry themselves looking for trouble, and hours are not sufficient for them when it comes to their examination, and they go through torments every time they go to confession. Their examination not only wearies them at the time of confession, but all day long. They are perpetually searching their conscience, and do nothing but fret and dissect themselves.

I admit that it is not easy to keep to the happy medium. For those who lead a regular life, with little contact with the outside world, whose occupations vary little, and who are in the habit of making their examination of conscience daily, I would say that the immediate preparation before confession should not take long: a glance should be sufficient to remind them of what they have done during the week. Persons otherwise circumstanced require more time, but such time has its limits. A quarter of an hour more than suffices for a weekly confession, and it is better to run the risk of forgetting some slight fault than to torture oneself in order to omit none.

The examination should be made simply, quietly and honestly, after having asked the Holy Ghost for that light on which you ought to rely rather than on your own research. Instead of making painful efforts to recall everything, beg the Holy Spirit to show you those faults which most displease God, which offend your neighbour, and hinder your own progress. Then think of those only which come to your mind. Pay more attention to habitual than to occasional faults, to those which are in any way deliberate than to such as are simply inadvertent.

But it is much more important to feel real contrition for sin, and to make an earnest resolution of amendment. Such souls as I have here in mind do not find this difficult as regards great sins, which I would imagine they hold in habitual abhorrence. But that is not the case with regard to lesser sins of omission or commission connected with propensities which they treat rather lightly, and against which they have not the courage to fight resolutely. Such are sins of vanity, curiosity, laziness, self- indulgence, censoriousness and so forth. Such sins are always cropping up, and it is not easy to conceive real sorrow for them, or to make up one's mind never to commit them again, so long as the root is left unattacked. What happens is that the branches are lopped off, but they grow again at once, because the root is spared. Contrition for venial faults, habitually and deliberately committed, is as suspect as that for mortal sins of the same nature. We would like to amend, but deep down our will is not so sure. Grace demands correction, but nature refuses.

It is true that we can only hope for moral certainty of our contrition, but if there is any way of quieting our minds on this point it is by forming an earnest resolution never to commit a fault deliberately and intentionally, and to keep to that resolution. Then nothing remains but faults of impulse, of inadvertence or simple frailty, to which the will only half consents. A firm resolution never to sin wilfully readily obtains from God the grace of sorrow for those sins into which we fall. For the work of repentance is not our own but the gift of God; and He only promises it to those who make good use of His other graces.

Doubt, then, O Christian soul, of the sincerity of your contrition until you have fully made up your mind to avoid every deliberate sin; but once this is your habitual disposition, then have no further uneasiness in the matter. You must not judge your contrition by the feelings that you endeavour to excite at the time of confession, nor by the acts you then make, but by your habitual hatred of sin, your degree of watchfulness against it, and your efforts to overcome evil propensities and habits. There is no rule but this, and this rule is safe.

You are alarmed sometimes, because you feel no sorrow for sin, and your heart seems frozen; your act of contrition appears to be a mere formal set of words. You used to feel really grieved; love constrained your heart, and you were even moved to tears. Look well within yourself. See if you do truly detest the sins you are going to confess. If so, be at ease, and seek no further assurance. Your state of mind is probably better than when you were touched with sensible grief. Do not hesitate, therefore, to cast aside all fears and doubts and scruples on this subject: and, having taken the advice of your confessor, if necessary, then dismiss the matter entirely from your mind.

Besides, we do not excite contrition, as some suppose, by squeezing feelings out of our hearts, or moving ourselves to tears, but by humbly asking God to inspire our souls with true repentance, and then simply and quietly making our act of contrition. It is enough to do so once before confession, repeating it while the priest is giving the absolution. Then as regards the accusation. This is very often defective. We either say too much, or too little, by reason of self-love or shame. Any defects which result from ignorance or natural stupidity, will be remedied by the confessor asking such questions as he deems fit.

The accusation should be short and simple. No useless details, which often implicate other people; no circumlocution. If you have to say that you were impatient, or wanting in charity, do not make a long story of it. Some people think they would make a bad confession, if they did not repeat exactly all that was said to them, and all that they said in reply.

It must be clear and precise. No indistinctness, ambiguity, or disguise. Let the confessor understand the thing as you do yourself. None of those vague accusations, which merely take up time, and to which those are prone who like to make long confessions. You accuse yourself of self-love and pride. But these are vicious habits; they are not sins. Of slackness in God's service: the exact way in which you are slack should be mentioned. You make lukewarm communions: what does that mean?

It must be thorough. No essential details should be suppressed. Together with the fault, mention the motive which induced it, and which is sometimes more sinful than the act itself. Be absolutely sincere. If any fault is particularly humiliating, or if you fear reproof for it, do not leave it to the last: really humble souls begin with these. It is good also to mention one's temptations, and explain in what they consist, even if you have reason to believe that you have not given way to them. Shame sometimes leads us to conceal certain temptations. There is danger in this. It is a device of the devil to render a fall easier, and it generally succeeds.

Lastly, the accusation must be strictly true. Do not exaggerate, diminish or excuse your faults. Call that certain which you believe to be certain; doubtful what you consider doubtful. Scrupulous persons and those who suffer from temptations are apt to accuse themselves of having consented when they have not done so. When the confessor knows his penitents well, he should be on his guard and not take them always at their word; otherwise, he may well drive them to despair. Others think they should say more rather than less: they should, if possible, say neither more nor less. Those who are possessed of a strong and lively imagination should be on their guard against it in their confessions.

Early instruction on the subject of confession is exceedingly important because, at a certain age, it is almost impossible to correct the erroneous customs contracted by long habit.

Except in cases of violent temptation and serious trouble, souls in the passive way examine themselves very quietly. They see the state of their conscience very clearly. They are neither scrupulous nor do they slur over anything, for God never fails to show them the least fault they commit. They are not uneasy in the matter of their contrition. They accuse themselves with childlike simplicity and candour. Their confessions are usually short and to the point. Unless obliged by rule, they only confess when they feel the need. When they do so by rule, they state quite simply that they have nothing on their minds, if that is the case. By these signs it is easy to know whether persons are in this way, or are disposed to enter it.

Some may ask whether it is advisable to make use of those exercises for confession and communion, which are to be found in most manuals of devotion. I consider them useful and even necessary for those who seldom approach the sacraments. They are suitable also for young people, who are trying to be good and find great difficulty in collecting their thoughts. Acts, well repeated, inspire devotion where it previously did not exist, and in general recall the mind from wandering. But I think that those who enjoy the blessing of frequent communion should acquire the habit of dispensing with these aids. For one thing, familiarity lessens their effect, and they are only striking when they are new. An exercise grows wearisome when we know it by heart, and it leaves us cold and dry. And so we go from one thing to another, without finding any real satisfaction.

Another great objection is that, when we find ready made acts in books, we make no effort to excite our hearts to make them ours, but having borrowed the sentiments of the writers fancy that we have expressed our own. And these feelings which are not our own leave very little behind them. Those, on the other hand, which come spontaneously from within us, with the help of grace, nourish the soul and develop it, giving rise to profitable dispositions and, by being frequently renewed, form a habit of interior recollection.

And there can be no doubt that the expression of our own feelings is much more pleasing to God, being the kind of prayer which comes straight from the heart. What can all these methodical and prearranged acts mean to God? The thoughts that really please Him are those which He Himself breathes into the soul, not those that we seek elsewhere. Provided they are not needed to make up for our indigence or fix our attention, it is better to do without them and leave the heart free to express itself to God in its own way. Free and spontaneous acts are much more natural and alive, and also more effective.

Therefore I would suggest that you try gradually to dispense with books, both before and after communion. Let your preparation and thanksgiving be made quietly, without any straining of the mind, and with the help of God alone, Who is never so near to us as in these holiest of acts. And while acknowledging the insufficiency of your own attempts to receive Jesus worthily, and worthily to thank Him for this inestimable benefit, I would wish you trustfully to ask Him to dispose your heart aright, and then firmly believe and fully expect Him to do so. Then remain quietly recollected and interiorly silent, giving Him complete liberty over your heart, both as to the preparation for His reception and to His taking entire possession of it.

This divine method in which Christ would give us of His fulness, and we would give Him our simplicity, humility, faith, love and trust, is much better than our bustle and activity, and the shakings we give our soul in order to produce a little sensible fervour. And what an intimate peace it brings; what sweet suspension of the powers of the soul; what loving expectation of Our Lord's coming and of the unspeakable blessedness of His presence. Our self-love is always wanting to have a finger in the business, and so spoils everything. It seems to fear that God cannot do as well as it can itself. Whenever self-love interferes, therefore, God does little or nothing.

I allow that this method is only suitable for souls that have made some progress. But there are pure, young hearts, and indeed wonderful penitents, whom God Himself calls to it, attracting them to an interior silence, and kindling in them a sweet, powerful love at the time of communion. These souls need fear nothing. At such times, let them leave aside not only books, but also their own acts, and yield to God's own action. The confessor need have no anxiety on this point.

It is true that sensible sweetness at communion lasts only a certain time, but it is also true that it should not be sought or clung to. Nor, when God withdraws it, should it be regretted. There is much spiritual sensuality in this: it is loving Our Lord, not for His own sake but for His consolations. When the privation of these consolations is not the result of any fault of ours, our communion is none the worse, although it may be devoid of comfort. Its peace is imparted, whether it be felt or no, and our heart is filled, however empty it may feel. Our state at communion generally corresponds to our state in prayer; and the further we advance in the mortification of self, the more are we weaned from all sweetness. If the heavenly food is then less pleasing to our taste, it is all the more strengthening. In its trials, it is strength that the soul needs, not consolations; and this strength is abundantly bestowed in those communions in which nothing seems to be imparted.

A communion is not to be judged by its immediate but by its subsequent effects. God soon leads strong and generous souls beyond sweetness, in order that He may give them what is more substantial. A communion is excellent when it results in a generous determination to correct our faults, to deny ourselves, to bear the internal and external crosses sent by God, and to give Him, according to our present state, the proofs He seeks of our love, faithfulness and abandonment. Communions which do not produce this effect bear very little fruit. Natural sensibility, the imagination (not to say the devil) may often have the chief share in the pleasure then enjoyed, which only serves to lull vain and timid souls into dangerous illusions.

Now as to frequent communion, the confessor should give his advice with holy discretion. It is the present mind of the Church that the practice of frequent and even daily communion should be encouraged for all Christians who are in a state of grace, and are led by a right and pious intention, namely by a sincere desire to advance in the spiritual life, and not by any human motive such as habit or vanity. As soon as a Christian sets himself diligently to work out his own salvation, he should be exhorted to communicate often, without waiting until he is entirely rid of his former habits, or rather in order that he may get rid of them more easily. And there may be reasons, such as occasions of strong temptations or difficult duties, which render frequent communion still more desirable.

Greater profit will, of course, accrue to those who are not attached to any venial sins, but are resolved to commit no intentional fault and to obey the will of God in all things; who, moreover, devote themselves to inward mortification and mental prayer, so far as their condition allows, in order to acquire strength in the practice of virtue, bravely fighting themselves and avoiding all that might in any way draw them away from their interior recollection and union with God. As the spiritual life has its normal rate of progress, it is always easy for an experienced director to see whether a soul is advancing or not, and he will advise the frequency of communion according to the needs of the penitent.

As for priests, secular or regular, who daily offer the Holy Sacrifice, they must never think any perfection too high for them. On the contrary, the priesthood is of itself an engagement to what is most perfect in the Christian life.

This is all the more so, when it is joined to the vows of religion. If one is obliged by one's office to say Mass, one is obviously obliged to say it worthily, and to draw from it all the spiritual fruits attached to it. It seems to me that by reason of their state, the functions they fulfil, and the example they should set, it is a law for them, not only to equal but to surpass in sanctity other Christians who live an interior life. But let each examine and judge himself in this matter.

Seventh Maxim: Purity of intention, simplicity and
uprightness

*Let your intention be pure, and your devotion simple and
upright.*

If thy eye be single, thy whole body shall be lightsome.
[32] All the Fathers explain these words to refer to purity of
intention, and understand them to signify that, if our aim be
pure, our actions will be just. As the eye guides, and in
some sense enlightens, the body, so the intention enlightens
the soul. It guides its actions, and imparts to them their
value for good or evil. Therefore, as the holiness of our
actions depends on the purity of our intention, it is of the
utmost importance that we should make sure of our
intention; yet nothing is more difficult.

Intention lies in the deepest part of the human heart, so
that, to discover it as fully as is possible, we must be
practised in the science of reflecting on our own soul,
examining its hidden motives, and penetrating its deepest
recesses. This is what few persons do, and in what concerns
supernatural matters it can only be satisfactorily performed
by the help of divine light, which must unceasingly be
sought by diligent prayer.

Our self-love endeavours studiously to hide our intentions
from ourselves. It does so with a view to its own interests,
and succeeds only too well. We deceive ourselves in a
multitude of things, and although we do so simply because
we want to, it is all so subtle that we are hardly aware of it.
There are very few persons who are completely honest with
themselves, and self should be the very first thing we
mistrust. We must always, therefore, be on our guard
against the devices of self-love, which are more subtle in

religious matters than in anything else. Yet how few are really watchful in this matter; how few are proof--I do not say always, but for the most part--against being taken off their guard.

If we are to know ourselves really, we must discern the true motive of our actions, and that is not an easy matter, seeing how twisted our nature is, and how blind we are to it. True knowledge of self is very rare.

The truth is, of course, that only God knows us through and through; above all in the most essential thing, namely whether we are worthy in His eyes of love or hatred. [33] We cannot be absolutely certain that any of our actions are pleasing to Him, and this uncertainty will remain with us all our life; we will never be able to pronounce with certitude on the purity of our intentions. For if we were sure on this point, we would be equally sure that our actions were holy, and consequently that we were in a state of grace. For this reason, we must always say with David: From my secret sins, cleanse me, O Lord. [34] And who knows fully his own frailty? The truth is in itself very painful, and particularly grievous to self-love, which is always seeking for assurance. According to God's designs, however, it should humble us, but not drive us to despair. If in this matter we cannot arrive at absolute certitude, yet by learning to know ourselves and by humbly asking it of God, we can obtain sufficient moral certitude to give us peace. But we must do all that lies in our power.

What, then, is purity of intention? Purity of intention is having God alone as our object, free from all self-interest. Yet our intention, although not absolutely pure, may not be fundamentally bad. It often happens that our primary intention is good, but it is spoilt by a secondary intention which is not good. Thus a priest in his apostolic work seeks in general the glory of God, but at the same time takes pleasure in the approbation of men. In God's eyes, therefore, which are infinitely pure, the total intention and the acts consequent on it, are not perfectly holy and beyond reproach.

Imperfect Christians that we are, we can judge by this example of the hidden imperfections which insinuate themselves into all we do. If only we were fully persuaded of this truth, how reluctant we would be to indulge in any self-complacency; and this is just what God wants, for He only saves us by humility, certainly not by confidence in our own merit. The saints knew this only too well, and like Job [35] trembled at the thought of their actions. And even St. Augustine cried, when he thought of Monica his mother: 'O my God, who can stand in Thy sight, if Thou searchest without mercy?'

What must we do to acquire this precious purity of intention? We must continually watch our motives, in order to eschew not only those that are obviously bad, but even those that are imperfect. But we only discern our imperfections as we advance, and as our spiritual light increases. God increases this light progressively, according to the use we make of His gift. He adapts it to our present needs, and to the degree of purity He expects of us at the time. It is by this light that we gradually discover those imperfections in our intention which at first were not apparent, and which God Himself actually hid from us. For what beginner, with how ever good a will, could bear the sight of those actions which he believes to be his best, if God showed them to him as they are in His sight? It would be enough to reduce him to the depths of despondency.

God has done so in the case of certain saints, but not everyone can stand such favours!

To make myself better understood, I will give an example of this imperfect knowledge of ourselves. The entrance to the spiritual life is often strewn by God with flowers. He fills the soul with sweetness and consolation in order to detach it from all that is not Himself, and to facilitate the exercises of an interior life, which otherwise would prove too difficult. The soul, which never before knew anything so delightful, clings impetuously to these new pleasures, and in order to enjoy them gives up everything else. It yields itself to prayer and mortification, and is only happy when alone with God. It cannot bear any interruption in its communion with Him. If God hides Himself for a time, it is wretched, and cries to Him to return. It seeks Him restlessly, and knows no rest until He is found again.

Much imperfection unquestionably exists here. The motive is good: God is the object sought; but the intention is not pure, because spiritual sweetness and sensible enjoyment are sought as well. The soul does not see this imperfection at the time; God Himself hides it, and it would be imprudent in a spiritual director to reveal it. But when the soul has for some time been fed on this milk, and begins to grow strong, the times of God's absence will grow longer, and will become habitual. Then a light will be given to show the previous imperfection in the intention, and the soul will gradually learn to serve God for Himself, and not for His gifts. This light would have done harm at first, but will be profitable when it is given. And at every new step fresh light is received, which reveals the imperfections of the preceding state. Therefore, instead of over-wearying ourselves by scrutinizing our intentions, we need only make good use of the light given us by God. Yet we must faithfully consult that light, and at once reject every imperfection which it makes known to us. And thus we gradually attain to a purity of intention which is more or less perfect, according to God's will concerning us. For purity of intention is the measure of holiness, and is proportionate to the degree of light communicated by God, and to the fidelity with which we correspond to it. God indeed considers, not our actions in themselves, but our motives. That is why the slightest action of Our Lady was of greater value in God's sight than the noblest works of other saints, because her intention was incomparably pure.

Simplicity is identical with purity of intention. Thus Our Lord said: If thy eye be single: [36] that is, if your gaze is directed to one object only, namely God. I could, therefore, be silent concerning simplicity, and content myself with what I have said concerning purity of intention. But it is desirable to show that simplicity, which so few persons rightly understand, is the root and essence of all perfection. To this intent, we must raise our minds to God Himself, and in the first place consider simplicity as it is revealed in Him.

Now only what is infinite is perfectly simple, and only what is perfectly simple is infinite. All things finite are manifold and complex, and all things complex are finite. There is no exception to this rule. Therefore, perfect simplicity can be postulated only of God, and that accounts for the infinity of His perfections. The being of God is infinite, because it is simple and all in all, without division or extension. His eternity is infinite, because it is simple, having neither beginning, middle nor end, and excludes the very idea of duration expressed by a succession of moments. His power is infinite, because it is simple, extending to all things possible, and exercised without contradiction or effort, by a pure act of will. His knowledge is infinite, because it is simple, and consists in one single idea, which is the idea of God Himself, in which He sees all that has been, is and will be, and all that is in the realm of mere possibility. The very essence of God is infinite, because it is simple. In Him essence is existence; His attributes are one with themselves and with His essence, being only distinguishable by the definitions we conceive of them, according to our own feeble imagination. In Him, finally, power means act, and faculty means exercise; divine intelligence an eternal understanding, and divine will an eternal volition.

So, too, in regard to His moral attributes. Although finite when viewed in their effects on us, they are infinite in themselves, by virtue of their simplicity. Such are His holiness, His wisdom, goodness, justice and mercy. The end of all His works is likewise infinite, being simple: it is to His glory that they must all concur. Minds accustomed to reflection will be able to follow the sublime theory which I here merely indicate.

Simplicity, then, being the chief characteristic of the perfections, designs and operations of God, we cannot wonder that it is the chief constituent of perfection in the case of rational creatures. Being finite, they are incapable of physical simplicity, but not of moral simplicity, and this they are bound to make their one aim.

In the case of the creature, simplicity is reduced to one point, namely that God alone is to be the standard of his ideas and judgments, the aim of his desires, and the end of his actions and sufferings. Everything is to be referred to God; His good pleasure is to be preferred in all things, His holy will alone to be envisaged, sought and pursued. This summary is short, but its content deep.

The soul is truly simple, when it has attained to this single view of God, and is perfected in unity. An ineffable unity, which in some sort deifies us by a most perfect moral union with Him Who is supremely and absolutely One. One to One was the continual saying of a great contemplative: a short expression, but full of meaning. It contains all the truth and perfection of holiness, all the blessedness of which it is the source. God is One by a unity which befits Him, and Him alone. He is One, and necessarily draws all things into His own unity. He is One, and sanctifies all things by participation in His unity. He is One, and all creatures capable of being happy are so only by sharing in His unity. Therefore, in order to be holy or happy, the soul must be one by its cleaving of mind and heart to Him alone, for Him alone, without any turning back towards self. If, besides looking to God, the soul gazes upon itself, in any way whatsoever distinguishing itself from God, with a sense of ownership which separates its interests from God's interests, then that soul is no longer one or simple, but double, having two objects. And as long as it is in this state, it cannot possibly be immediately united to God, neither in this world by faith, nor hereafter until it has been purified of all its multiplicity.

Therefore, if you would aspire to holiness and happiness, aspire to simplicity and unity. Study to simplify your desires, reducing them to God alone. Forget yourself, think of Him; have no will nor interest but His. Seek only His glory, and find your happiness in His. This is the state of the blessed in heaven, and we shall only be admitted to the beatific vision with all its beatitude when we have arrived at that consummation. Why not, then, begin on earth, so far as we can?

But how are we to acquire this simplicity, the mere idea of which transcends all our conceptions? First, we must pray to the Being Who alone is infinitely holy, and ask Him to undertake the work of our simplification. Let this be our great, our sole aim. All our efforts will never rid us of our multiplicity. But the more God acts in us, and the more we yield to the operations of grace, the more shall we increase in simplicity, without seeing, or even wanting to see, the progress we are making.

In what are we to seek simplicity? In our mind: from which God will banish much prejudice and uncertainty, many doubts and false judgments, substituting in their place the simple truth, and from which in turn He will drive away all undue worrying, misgivings, want of trust and cares for the future, which are the consequences of a false prudence. Thus will He gradually reduce our multifold reasonings to the prayer of simple regard.

Simplicity in our will, which will henceforth own but one desire, one fear, one love, one hatred, and one sole object of its affection, drawing us ever nearer to that object, with an inviolable rectitude and an unconquerable strength.

Simplicity in virtues, which will all meet and fuse in charity, so far as the state of this present life permits. Simplicity in prayer, which will be, so to speak, one only act containing all acts in itself. And lastly, simplicity in conduct, which will be consistently even, uniform, straight and true, emanating from one principle and culminating in one end.

Uprightness is but another name for purity of intention and simplicity. Of this I would speak but briefly.

The Sacred Word, speaking of Job, found no higher praise than to call him simple and upright. [37] A man is upright, when he follows a simple rule pointing always in one direction, and aiming always at a centre. For the soul, this centre is God; and God has given it an innate tendency towards Himself. So long as it preserves and obeys this tendency, it will retain its innocence and peace; departing from it, it cannot fail to fall back into sin and distress. It does this when it turns back on itself, assuming another direction and another centre, thereby losing its primitive rectitude. It was given an original impulse, but has chosen another and in an opposite direction, which in devious ways draws it away from God and towards self.

Again, Scripture tells us: God made man upright: [38] that is, turned towards Himself alone, with an inward yearning for closeness to and union with Him. But owing to his radical imperfection man had the power of turning towards himself, and he was tempted and fell. Thence arose original sin and its consequences, which gave a prodigious impetus to this tendency towards self, and to which, without God's recalling grace, we cannot but yield.

I am aware that as long as man retains sanctifying grace, he does not lose that essential uprightness which is necessary and sufficient for salvation. But every act of self-love, of self- complacency, of seeking one's own interest unsubordinated to the interest of God, is a deflection from that uprightness which, however slight, may entail the most grievous consequences. The danger of the least error of this kind is twofold. First, we can never, by our own strength, regain our former uprightness, however slightly we may have diverged from it. Secondly, we have no power of stopping, nor of carrying our deflection to a given point and no further. These two considerations ought to weigh with us so deeply as to prevent our ever taking one deliberate step out of the right way.

Try to preserve, then, as far as you can, that rectitude which God has restored to you. Fear its loss, even in the smallest degree. Keep a watch over your natural tendencies, which would draw you away from God. In this, we are our worst enemies, loving ourselves but in a wrong way, with a secret inclination to make self our centre, towards which we try to make everything, even God Himself subservient. This love of self is extremely dangerous, because its devices are so subtle that often enough we are not aware of them, so deeply embedded are they in our nature. Life to self is death to the soul, since it is taking us always farther from God.

Wise will we be if we examine well the nature of our devotion, to see if it be pure, simple and straight. And as it is possible that we are blind to ourselves, we should pray about it, seek counsel, and profit by the light God gives us. The good use we make of the little we have will draw down still greater graces, and insensibly we shall acquire that purity of intention and simplicity and uprightness of heart which are, and always have been, so rare among those who profess to be devout.

31.   Cf. Matt. v. 24
32.   Matt. vi. 22

33.   Cf. Eccles. IX,!

34.   Ps. xviii. 13

35.   Cf. Job xxxvii, 1

36.   Matt. vi. 22

37.   Job 1:1

38.   Eccles. vii:30

Eighth Maxim: The natural spirit and the spirit of Christ

*Follow the enlightening spirit of Christ: mistrust the
blindness and treachery of the natural mind.*

Most devout persons are religious after their . own fashion
and according to their own ideas, and character. The
number of those who, denying themselves thoroughly, seek
to follow no light but that of grace, and willingly deny
themselves their own light that they may be enlightened by
eternal wisdom, is very small indeed. The practical
application of this maxim, on which depends almost all
progress in the interior life, is much more difficult for men
than for women, because men trust more to their own
judgment. If you were to suggest to a man full of
confidence in his own reason and good sense, that he
should give up his private judgment in order to enter into
the ways of God, he would not understand you, nor would
he see the necessity of what you propose. He cannot
conceive that God's thoughts are higher than our thoughts,
and His ways other than our ways. [39] He believes that he
has the right to guide himself, and the power to guide
others.

What is the result? He will never be thoroughly subjected
to the divine spirit. He will contradict it, fight against it,
both in himself and in those for whom he may be
responsible. He will form false judgments concerning
spiritual things and persons. He will obstinately reject what
is good, and approve what is harmful, or else vacillate
between one and the other; so that there is nothing fixed or
consecutive either in his principles or direction.

What, then, is the natural spirit, or the spirit of private judgment? It is human reason in so far as it professes to judge of the things of God by its own light, without recourse to the light of grace. It is natural prudence, which conceives itself all sufficient, and is ready to propose maxims and rules of conduct, both for itself and for others, without consulting God or those who stand in His place.

Now in order to grasp this fully, we must lay down as a first principle that we do not really know the secrets of the interior life, nor all that pertains to the operations of grace except by a supernatural light: that our ideas on these things are only correct in so far as God impresses them on our souls, and that by this means alone do we rightly understand what is written concerning them in Holy Scripture, and in books treating of such matters. Without that light, it is impossible to distinguish, in ourselves or in others, between what comes from God and what emanates from other sources. Hence it follows that, if we are to form right judgments in these matters, our reason must be in continual dependence on the spirit of God, and fully persuaded of its own insufficiency and complete incompetence. It must have constant recourse to prayer; or, rather, it must be in a state of continual prayer.

It also follows that a true acquaintance with the secrets of the interior life can never be acquired merely by reading books, however exact and profound they may be; nor by the kind of meditation in which one simply relies on one's own reflections. We must have light from above, and this is only possible by humble prayer. Otherwise, we will understand nothing of what we read; or, if by presumption we imagine we understand something, it will be all wrong. In general, anyone who is not leading an interior life will not really understand spiritual things, or be able to make a profitable use of what he understands. And even those who are in the interior way will only appreciate in books what they have learnt from experience. Anything beyond that will be unintelligible to them, unless God gives them the light. And since God wants to lead us by the obscure way of faith, He generally does not give us this light for ourselves, but rather to those who are our guides in this matter.

Now this knowledge, being infused, is only to be retained by humility, by faithful correspondence with grace, and by a continual care to advance in holiness. It is lost if pride appropriates it to itself; if prayer and other salutary exercises are neglected; if too much play is allowed to reasoning and curiosity; if a curb is not kept on the activity of the mind. The mind must be passive if it is to receive what God has to give. Nothing is more delicate than the spirit of God. It is infinitely pure, and will brook no interference from the purely natural spirit. Nothing is more difficult than to receive and preserve it in all its purity, so inclined are we to insinuate something of our own into it. Nothing requires more attention, more watchfulness, more distrust of self. Self-love and the devil make it their one business to abuse and ruin it in our hearts, to turn us away from it, and deprive us of it by secret and imperceptible devices.

A whole volume would be necessary to describe fully this spirit of private judgment: to define its distinctive characteristics, and to tell of its fatal consequences, both for ourselves and for others. It is the oldest malady of the soul, and was the first step in original sin in the case of our first parents. They would not have sinned, had they not called in question God's commandment; had they not searched for the motive of His prohibition, and listened to the tempter's suggestion. The purely natural spirit taught them to scrutinize, and led them to disobey. To it they owed the loss of their original rectitude, simplicity and happy innocence, and their fatal acquaintance with evil, hitherto unknown to them.

Now this malady is the most universal, the most deeply-seated and inveterate, and the most difficult of all to cure. It is a subtle poison, corrupting the whole substance of the soul, and infecting even its good qualities and virtues. It is the enemy of God and of His grace. It forbids entrance to His gifts, or robs men of them. All sins committed are either its effect or its punishment. Ordinary grace is not enough for its cure: it resists the most violent remedies, and calls for very special grace. Its cure demands long and acute trials, and so long as life lasts we cannot be sure that it is eradicated. One glance at self may be sufficient to revive it in the noblest of souls; death alone frees us from it for ever.

Self-will is another misery which, according to St. Bernard, opened hell, and follows on the heels of the purely natural spirit. It is, so to say, its offspring, for our judgments precede and determine our affections. If the heart clings to objects from which the mind warns it to turn, or if it feels an aversion for what the mind indicates that it should love, it is because then the mind is being guided, not by private judgment, but by an enlightened reason or by supernatural grace, both of which come from God. So the fact remains that, not only deliberate sins but sins of frailty or surprise are all children of the purely natural spirit, from which we see how dangerous the latter is, and how very much on our guard we must be in regard to it.

The marks by which it is known would be easily recognized if seen by other eyes than our own. We have no difficulty in perceiving them in others, and are only too ready to do so. But the signs we notice in others we are blind to in ourselves.

This private spirit is self-confident, presumptuous, argumentative, over-bold and quick to judge. It is stubborn and unwilling to give way, so imbued is it with a sense of its own importance. It wants to see, and is loath to bend itself under the yoke of authority, which would have it believe. It is curious and must know everything. It does not perceive its own limits, and, presuming all things to be within its own depth, ventures to fathom all. It dare not claim to be infallible, but acts as if it were. To admit itself in the wrong is its greatest humiliation. The more one seeks to convince it, the more opinionated it becomes. And even when it is proved to be in the wrong, it refuses to yield. Through sheer obstinacy it shuts its eyes to what is known to be true.

And yet its sight is imperfect. It does not accepl things as they are, but views them in the light most flattering to itself. It is deceitful, false, perverse, haughty, censorious and contemptuous. It fears humiliation as it loves praise, and is continually adding secretly to the adulation it receives. It is mistrustful, suspicious, ready to believe evil and to doubt good, and to give a bad interpretation to the most innocent things. It is self- satisfied, never pleased with others unless praised by them, always holding them to be in the wrong as soon as they begin to contradict or blame.

Such, and still more horrible, are the characteristics of the purely natural spirit. It would be shocked, could it see itself as it is. But the crowning point of its misery lies in that it is blind, and its wilful blindness increases by reason of its deformity. If you endeavour to open its eyes, you irritate and excite it; it rebels against you, and all you say in order to undeceive it merely confirms it in its self-complacency.

The reason is that, blind as it is, it fancies itself clear-sighted. The more it is mistaken with regard to itself, the more certain it feels that it does itself a justice which is refused it by others. Its blindness arises from the fact that it sees itself only in the false glare of pride, vanity and presumption, which not only hides its vices and defects, but gives them the appearance of virtues. If it should consult objective reason, and still more grace, it would know itself truly by means of this dual light. But it never does, and inasmuch as it is a purely natural spirit, it is incapable of doing so.

In speaking thus, I depict almost all men, even those who profess to be pious and good, not excepting even a great number of those who think themselves interior and spiritual souls. This spirit of private pride, as regards religion, is exactly the same thing as the spirit of the Pharisees, of which Our Lord drew so striking a picture in the Gospels, which He attacked so strenuously in His discourses, and condemned so openly by His example. He even consented to be its victim, in order the more thoroughly to deter His disciples from it.

And yet, unfortunately, this Pharisaism is very common among pious folk of all conditions. There are those who, in the exercise of their calling seek for temporal advantages and the good opinion of men. They welcome the rich and great of this world with open arms and flattering words, while they will have nothing to do with the lowly and poor, or treat them harshly. They exercise despotic rule over men's consciences, make a show of the utmost rigour and severity, exaggerate and condemn, and see sin in everything. They are slaves to external practices, and recognize only the letter and nothing of the spirit. They have a set routine of prayers, and make artificial bounds for themselves, which they would not dream of overstepping. They criticize others, setting themselves up as living examples to be followed. Blind to their own faults, they are for ever looking for defects in others.

There are also those who, knowing only their own dry form of meditation, despise simple and humble prayer which, they say, is a waste of time and dangerously like laziness. Others again feign a kind of stiff out-of-the-way spirituality, full of affectation, the seat of which is certainly not in the heart but in a proud mind and a deluded imagination.

At the bottom of all this is the fact that these people have substituted their own private spirit for the spirit of God; or, at least, it is all so involved that they will never make any real progress. What is more, they bring discredit on true piety, and scandalize worldly folk who are thus disgusted with religion, holding it responsible for a jumble which in fact it utterly condemns.

The first thing to be resolved by anyone who sets out to lead a truly Christian life and to discard from his devotions all the faults I have just mentioned is, not only to mistrust his private spirit but to study how to rid himself of it. He must fight against it and pursue it relentlessly. This spiritual combat forms the main part of that denial of self which Our Lord enjoins on all who seek to follow Him. [40]

But the private spirit cannot fight against itself, because it does not know itself. Reason, unless enlightened by faith and aided by grace, is but a feeble weapon. We know of no case of any philosopher, who by his own deliberations ever succeeded in ridding himself of his private spirit. The slight conquests won in that way, far from weakening it, only supply it with fresh vigour by reason of the vain complacency it derives from its triumphs. The only way to master it is to engage it with the arms of grace, and to beg God to take the matter into His own all-powerful hands. It must be handed over to God as His mortal enemy, protesting that its utter destruction will be hailed as the greatest of blessings. If this prayer is sincere and often repeated, God will certainly take over the battle, while instructing us how to fulfil our part. He will endow us with His own spirit, and we shall quickly be aware of its presence. His spirit will gradually undermine and regulate our own activity. It will cause its deliberations to cease, quieten its agitations, correct its wrong notions, lessen its malignity, crush its pride, and overcome its egoistic bent. Then it will not be long before we can say with St. Paul: I live, now not I, but (the spirit of) Christ liveth in me. [41]

How is all this to be brought about? That is God's secret, so utterly inexplicable that the human spirit cannot penetrate it, and will never die if it attempts to do so. It can only die in so far as it allows itself to be deprived in turn of every private judgment, of every private act, of every private feeling. What I can say is that we soon begin to perceive the effects of the work of grace. We feel ourselves to be a totally different person, and we know that the cause of the change is the interior spirit communicated to us by God. But what that interior spirit is, and how it works, we do not know.

The change at once produced by it in our ideas and affections is such that it has to be experienced to be understood. Holy Scripture speaks of it as the birth of the new man: an inward, spiritual man who, by his gradual development, imperceptibly destroys the old man and, arrived at his full strength, slays him utterly. The food of this new man is prayer, infused prayer, continued almost unceasingly so long as reason retains its sway, and resumed on waking after the night's sleep. It is prayer, interior, yet, so to speak, without our own act; which, once it becomes habitual, maintains itself.

This is the unobtrusive weapon we are to bring to bear upon the purely private spirit. Its work is furthered by temptations, trials, contradictions and humiliations. God employs all these means to quell so formidable an enemy, even the prejudices and wickedness of men, the malice of Satan, and the threatening arms of His own justice. So Job says: The terrors of the Lord war against me. [42] The soul seconds God in this war by yielding itself to His crucifying operations, adding to these its own practices of interior mortification.

It will readily be allowed that the natural or private spirit is as I have described it: blind, deceitful and treacherous, and that we must follow the spirit of Jesus, which alone prevents us from walking in darkness and gives us the light of life. No doubt all who would faithfully serve God intend to follow His spirit, but why, it will be asked, do so few do so in reality?

I would suggest that the number of those who sincerely desire to serve God is not so great as is commonly supposed. Not because we are hypocrites, or that we want to deceive others, but because we deceive ourselves. If we were really honest, would we flatter ourselves, spare ourselves, withhold from God so many things that we know He is asking of us? Would we turn a deaf ear to grace and complain of its importunity; use every device to deafen our conscience and try to fit God's interests in with our own? Do we not know that God requires of every Christian that he deny himself in all things and always? [43] And yet, do we do so? What does the voice of conscience say to us in this matter; or rather what does it say to God?

And so I aver that the intention men entertain of the following of Christ is for the most part vague and speculative and not really deep. It is indeterminate, it does not spring from the depths of the will, and is rarely maintained in practice. Yet if we are to follow the spirit of Christ we must know that spirit. It must be studied, and that means entering into the mind of Christ, searching out, as the Imitation says, the sentiments and dispositions of His soul. Who are those who make the interior of Jesus their habitual dwelling place? And still more, who are those who put into practice what they learn there, and recognize no half measures in their determination to conform themselves to the mind of Christ? [44] Such Christians are indeed rare.

Most persons have not even the slightest idea of the spirit of Jesus. Others are afraid of knowing too much about it, because they know they would have to conform their lives to it. Others are willing to imitate (but how imperfectly) some of its features, but will not walk with Him the whole way.

What really was the mind of Christ; the spirit which gives us light, and guides us in the way of salvation? It was a perfectly interior spirit, by which He was constantly united to the Father, entirely devoted to His glory and to His good pleasure. It was a spirit lifted infinitely beyond all perishable pleasures, riches and honours, leading Him to choose and embrace poverty and obscurity, toil and suffering, humiliations and opprobrium in the extreme. [45] It was a spirit detached from all natural affections and feelings, always and in all things dependent upon grace, and so submissive to its workings as never to think or will or desire or do anything apart from it. It was a spirit over which the divinity, to which His humanity was hypostatically united, exercised perfect sway, boundless authority, and a constant influence. It was a spirit which never permitted Him to think of His own interests, His own glory. It attributed nothing to Himself, and never permitted Him one glance of self-complacency to the unique and infinite dignity to which He was raised by the hypostatic union, but which He maintained in a state of perfect devotedness to His Father's interests, [46] of unreserved sacrifice to the claims of divine justice, of utter humility, and continual self-effacement.

This is the spirit of Christ which, as Christians, we are bound to make our own. [47] It is in this respect, above all, that as head of the elect Jesus is given to us as our model. God wanted to show us in Him what we ought to be. It was as our example that the eternal Word deigned to assume our nature, and if we would be His disciples we must follow in His steps. [48] Some persons excuse themselves by saying that Jesus was God. But it is not as God but as man that He offers Himself for our imitation. We shall never attain to the perfections of the divine original: we know that, and it would be impiously absurd to try to do so. But all must endeavour to respond to the graces given them, just as Jesus responded to His. That is all God asks; but He also asks no less.

It may also be suggested that because Jesus was God everything was easy to Him, that it cost Him nothing. It is true that He could not sin, nor could He resist grace. It is also true that He found no obstacle within Him to any virtue whatsoever. But it is also true that He habitually endured sufferings infinitely more distressing than those of all the martyrs and saints put together, and this because His human nature was overwhelmed and crushed under the terrible weight of the divine justice. As God-man He certainly felt and suffered all that a God-man could feel and suffer. God does nothing in vain, and in the great design of the Incarnation and the redemption of mankind, all was ruled and measured by infinite wisdom and justice. What the Father required of the Son was proportioned to the grace and strength given Him.

Yet if the sight of so perfect a pattern terrifies us in our cowardice, let us turn our eyes on mere men. On St. Paul, for instance, who called on Christians to be followers of him as he was of Christ. [49] Study the mind of the apostle in his epistles, and seek to make it a model for your own conduct. You will tell me that he was a man converted by an extraordinary grace, a chosen vessel, concerning whom God had special designs, and on whom He lavished His gifts. I would answer that St. Paul was sanctified neither by his apostleship nor by his election. He was sanctified by his correspondence with God's grace, and it is in this, and this only, that you are asked to imitate him. What is there to hinder you? Was not St. Paul a blasphemer and a persecutor when God threw him to the ground? When grace, then, calls to you, say as he said: Lord, what wilt Thou have me to do? [50] And then do the bidding of grace as faithfully as he did.

Would you have patterns more within your reach? Then read the lives of the saints, of all ages, of all ranks, and of all conditions. Many retained their baptismal innocence; other had been great sinners, subject to the same passions, the same habits, the same temptations as ourselves, and often greater. They had as many or more obstacles to surmount, and it is remarkable that the Church never won more saints than in those early ages when to profess Christianity was a pledge of martyrdom.

But you will complain that they were saints. What other models would you have? What are you called to, except to sanctity such as theirs? They were sanctified only because they were true disciples of Jesus Christ, and by following the spirit, the teaching and the example of their Master.

But whence do these vain objections come? From our purely natural spirit, and nothing reveals more clearly how blind it is. In all the imitative arts, it is always the best models that are sought, studied with the greatest care, and painstakingly copied. Why should we complain, then, in this most important of all the arts that our models are too perfect when what is at stake is the right conduct of our lives, and our well-being in God's eyes, which is to make us worthy of His eternal possession? What a contradiction! We refuse to put on the spirit of Christ, because it means putting off our own. But so long as men will not give up their purely natural spirit or the spirit of private judgment they must give up the idea of being true Christians. For there is no genuine and practical Christianity except that which consists in thinking and acting in conformity with the spirit of Christ.

39.   Isaias lv. 8
40.   Cf Luke ix:23
41.   Gal. ii.20
42.   Job vi. 4
43.   Cf. Matt. xvi. 24
44.   Cf. Phil. ii. 5
45.   Cf. Phil. ii. 8
46.   Cf. John xiv. 31
47.   Cf. Phil. ii. 5
48.   I Peter ii. 21
49.   I Cor. xi. 1
50.   Acts ix. 6

Ninth Maxim: The outward and inward man

Take no account of external things: seek strenuously after those blessings which are to be found within.

The natural man, the old or fallen man, is called the outward man on account of his natural bias towards objects of sense. The spiritual man, the new man, or the man according to grace, is called the inward man because, dwelling apart in himself with God, he cleaves only to things that are invisible and supernatural.

Sensible objects hold an extraordinary sway over man. Their power begins in childhood, when pleasures and pain take their rise from these sources alone. It develops with age. The soul is keenly affected by all that strikes it from without; admiration and envy are excited by those accidents which raise some persons above their fellows, such as nobility, office, honours and wealth. Men look on these things as truly good, they bestow esteem and love upon them, seek only to enjoy them, and believe that happiness lies in the possession, and misery in the absence, of these advantages.

The work of sense and of corrupt nature is already far advanced, when grace comes forward to destroy it, and raise a very different structure upon its ruins. Grace teaches us that we are true Christians only in so far as we despise sensible things and turn to those of the spirit, by ceasing to be outward and becoming wholly inward men.

It follows, then, that the Christian who lives an interior life at intervals and, as it were, by fits and starts, is not perfect, while the perfect Christian is so in all things and at all times. To aim at an interior life and at Christian perfection are one and the same thing.

This is a hard lesson for nature to learn. Some refuse to accept it at all, others listen impatiently and resist as long as they can and, when they do put it into practice, do so grudgingly and with great repugnances Only a few learn this wisdom, and even these pass through long and painful struggles in acquiring it. This heavenly wisdom is utterly different from that of the world; indeed, it costs a great deal to rise to so noble a view of life.

The Christian is, in this respect, a being of another world; intended, not only for immortality but for eternal happiness in God; a happiness which surpasses all his thoughts, all his aspirations and hopes, even the very exigence of his nature. It is the pure gift of God, promised by revelation, and known only by faith.

We are prepared for this end by other blessings of the same order, which we call graces. The chief of these is habitual and is called sanctifying grace. The others are actual, and tend either to regain sanctifying grace if it is lost, or to preserve and increase it. The object of these graces is to raise to the supernatural order, both the state of the Christian and his free acts by which alone he can merit the possession of God.

The Christian is born into this world, and dwells herein for a certain time. But he is not of the world: it is not his; he is a stranger and a sojourner in it. Present and sensible objects are not his object. He may use them, as St. Augustine says, but not enjoy them. That is, God grants them to him for the necessities of his animal life, but his heart must not cling to them nor rest in them as in its final end. The true riches of the Christian on earth are grace, close communion with God, and all that fosters the supernatural life within him. Those things only are real evils which weaken that life, or deprive him of it.

External good and evil, therefore, are to him, properly speaking, neither really good nor really bad. But things called good may become evil, and the reverse, according to the use he makes of them. It is not so with interior good and evil. These are essentially connected with his supernatural state: that is, with his state as a Christian, and his eternal happiness or the contrary.

Consequently he ought to be indifferent to sensible good and evil, because in themselves they are indifferent things, which are profitable or harmful according to his interior dispositions. On the other hand, the whole strength of his mind and will must be devoted to the acquirement of such good and the avoidance of such evil things in the supernatural order, which can never be indifferent to him because of their intimate connection with his last end.

All Christians are much of one mind touching this great truth, so far as theory is concerned; but almost all follow other principles in practice. I am not here alluding to those who crave passionately for wealth, honours and pleasures, and who consider all means as lawful whereby their desires can be satisfied. These are Christians only in name, and so long as they continue in such a frame of mind, they can have no claim to being so in deed.

But among the rest, are there not many who are proud of their condition in life; who, having it in their power to aspire to honours and dignities, hanker after them, do all they can to procure them, feel delighted when their plans succeed, and miserable when they fail? And so with many other things.

Take riches alone. I pass over the countless numbers in all ranks of life who amass them by means which probity, to say nothing of our faith, condemn, and concerning which there is so much deceit. But I ask: are there many Christians who, having all they need to support their families in decency and sufficiency, wish for nothing more? Are they not always fancying that they have not enough? And is it not true that where you have opulence you will find pride, and with an increase of wealth an increase of self- esteem?

Then as regards pleasures, even those that are lawful (for I speak not of others): is there not much sensuality, solicitude and fastidiousness to be found even among Christians? Are not these pleasures eagerly sought, and jealously enjoyed? Are they not even invented, varied and multiplied with consummate skill? How careful men are to surround themselves with comforts, to avoid all that is disagreeable. How they flatter their body, and bestow on it all the gratification for which it is so ravenous. People think that they are very good Christians if, in these matters, they keep within the letter of the law, and run into no excess. But that is very different from the attitude of a perfect Christian.

The perfect Christian stifles the slightest germ of ambition in his heart. Not only does he not desire honours, but he fears them, abhors and shuns them, remembering the words of the Gospel: For that which is high to men is an abomination before God. [51] He sees in positions of dignity nothing but a burden for his conscience, heavy duties to be fulfilled, and grave responsibilities to be answered for. Should birth or Divine Providence call him to such posts, he appears in the simple garb of modesty and humility. He is ever watchful over himself and against the snares that are prepared for him on all sides. He continually examines his conduct with the most scrupulous attention, deeming himself answerable for all the good he fails to do, as for the evil he does not hinder. If he is of low estate, he thanks God and rejoices in it as being a state more conformable to the Gospel, happier and more innocent and more conducive to his salvation, and makes no attempt to change it. Not only does he hate honours but he seeks humiliations, for he knows and appreciates their value. If they befall him, he receives them as favours from heaven, and considers himself happy if he is despised, opposed, slandered and persecuted like his Master.

Then again, the true Christian, taught by the Gospel, looks upon riches as thorns and encumbrances which turn him away, in spite of himself, from more important cares. He possesses them without clinging to them, uses them with extreme moderation, shares them with the poor, whose steward he regards himself. He cuts down his expenses as much as possible in their favour, convinced that his excess is their need, and that all that he can spare belongs to them. If he is poor, he rejoices in his poverty, is glad to feel its effects, and even to want sometimes for necessities. Nor would he change his position even if he could. He esteems it too great a privilege thus to bear some resemblance to his Lord, Who chose to be born, and to live and die, poor.

The holy severity of the Gospel is his rule of conduct in the matter of pleasures. He seeks none for their own sake, and passes through natural and necessary gratifications as through fire. In no respect will he indulge the flesh, but mortifies it ingeniously, giving no quarter to predilections and overcoming repugnances, but all with holy liberty, unaffectedly and with discretion. No saint, that is no true Christian, ever indulged his body, and most have sought to bring it into subjection by fastings, vigils and mortifications generally, which today would terrify our self-indulgence and cowardice. They all considered it an essential duty to bear about them, in their body, the mortification of Jesus. [52]

Such, with regard to this world's goods, have perfect Christians always been, even when living in the world; for I do not restrict what I have said to those who have embraced voluntary poverty and chastity, and have left the world to live in solitude and in monasteries. In whatever state they were born, and wherever God placed them, they applied themselves to die to their body, and to refuse it even the most innocent satisfaction. Being faithful to grace, they set no bounds to their generosity.

Let not those be alarmed at this picture who, as St. Bernard says, see only the cross they have to bear and not the unction it brings. Let them not fancy that a true Christian's life is one of perpetual torture and restraint. The licentious and impious love to depict it under these frightening colours, to justify their having turned their backs on it; but they blaspheme what they know not, and deceive themselves of set purpose, and want to deceive others too.

No. The true Christian, in following the moral law, is not disturbed or worried. He does, indeed, do violence to his nature, but not to his mind or heart. He is perfectly convinced that he ought to do what he does, and he is glad to do it. If he despises, hates and shuns the delights and false pleasures on which he has turned his back, it is from a supernatural motive. God has raised him above all that. He has shown him the true nature of such things, and that knowledge prevents him from seeing in them anything but vanity and vexation of spirit. [53] In the school, first of wisdom then of experience, the Christian learns that to serve God is to reign; that to possess virtue is wealth, and that true joy consists in peace of mind.

It is by turning our thoughts inwards to our soul, and by learning from our past errors; it is in the silence of meditation and prayer, that we make the wonderful discovery that true happiness is not to be found in the things of the world. It is there we perceive the nothingness of earthly things, and realize that they are capable, indeed, of exciting our passions but never of satisfying our heart. There a deep secret touch of grace tells us that our true happiness lies in God alone: that in order to enjoy and possess Him we must give up all other joys, or at least our clinging to them. Henceforth, all things seem insipid except prayer and communion with God. The world is crucified to us, and we to the world. [54] We are drawn to God alone. We have sought Him and found Him in the sanctuary of our own soul. [55]

How shall we express our delight at having found within ourselves what we have vainly sought elsewhere? How shall we tell of our joy at discovering the real, infinite and inexhaustible treasure, which alone is capable of filling the immense capacity of our heart, or rather for which the heart is too small, and wherein it plunges and loses itself? After having experienced this happiness, how is it possible to think of leaving God and returning to created things, forsaking the Fountain of living waters for broken cisterns that can hold no water; [56] to hover between God Who is all and things that are naught; to prefer the bitter waters to the sweet; to risk the loss of the substance of our true happiness for the vain shadow?

It is not possible. At least, it is only possible if, with unheard-of infidelity, we little by little leave the interior way upon which we had entered. We may continue to make our meditations, and even to make them well, all the time keeping up some connection with the senses and with the things that please them. What we cannot do is to give ourselves to contemplative prayer without severing, so for as we can, our intercourse with created things; for the essence of such prayer is to concentrate all our affections on God, allowing no love but what is through Him, in Him and for Him.

Make the attempt, O Christian soul, and you will see that I speak truly. If you tell me that it is not within your power to enter upon this way of prayer, I answer in God's Name that He is ready to second your good will, and that He will introduce you into it, if you will do your part. Have at least the good will; and, since we cannot be sure even of that, ask it of God earnestly. That prayer alone is a good beginning; and how can God refuse you what He inspires you to ask? If few possess it, it is because few desire it; and those who do ask, ask often in fear of being heard! God reads the heart, and He sees whether we respond to His advances, and He never fails to cooperate when we do; but not otherwise. We may reproach Him with turning a deaf ear to our prayers. We protest that we have prayed in vain, that it is useless that we ask for a good will: He does not give it. The day will come, however, when God will make it clear to us that we have only ourselves to blame, if this is so. I do repeat: a soul that cooperates to the best of its ability to present grace must infallibly receive still greater graces according to its increasing needs; and if it perseveres, it will arrive at the degree of sanctity that God intends for it.

51.   Luke xvi. 15
52.   Cf 2 Cor. iv. 10
53.   Cf. Eccles. I. 14
54.   Cf. Gal. vi. 14
55.   Cf. Cant. iii. 4
56.   Jer. ii. 13

Tenth Maxim: Recollection, active and passive

Listen to Him Who teaches the heart without sound of words. Receive His peace, and guard it faithfully.

The delights of God are to be with the children of men. He loves to speak to the heart of man. Hence the secret of the spiritual life consists in knowing how to retire into one's own heart, and dwell therein with God. How does God convert sinners? By calling them to enter into their own hearts, where, their sins appearing before their eyes, they experience the greatest remorse, salutary thoughts arise in their minds, and they are filled with good intentions. If they do not shrink from dwelling within themselves, if they do not flee from themselves and seek relief or diversion in external objects, a change will soon take place in their lives.

If a soul is well meaning but unsettled, frivolous, prone to many faults, clinging to certain venial sins; or, if having once been fervent it has fallen into lax ways, God makes use of these same means to draw it away from its imperfections, and restore it to its former zeal. He calls it into itself. There it hears His reproaches and realizes that they are just and severe, yet gentle. If it listens with a docile spirit, it will make progress, and if it continues thus dwelling within itself with God, it will infallibly advance from virtue to virtue. [57]

This turning within to listen to the voice of grace is called recollection. This term expresses the act whereby the soul gathers and collects into itself those powers of attention hitherto scattered and divided among many objects. There are two kinds of recollection: the one which is active and is the work of the will aided by grace, and the other which is passive and is the gift of God. The latter is usually the reward of the former, after it has been faithfully practised over a period of time.

The first object of active recollection is the custody of the senses, especially of sight and hearing, which are, as it were, the windows through which the soul looks out and busies itself with passing things. When the soul is thus for the most part attentive to all that is going on outside itself, it cannot keep watch within, nor give heed to the interior Master, Who seeks to instruct and correct it: it cannot so much as hear His words.

Therefore it is necessary to accustom oneself to exercise great restraint over one's eyes, so as to acquire the power of turning them, not only from dangerous but from distracting and diverting objects. By restraining the restless mobility of the eyes, we at the same time quieten the levity and moderate the vivacity of the imagination. Passion is checked at its source, and the soul is wonderfully disposed to meditation, and still more to silent prayer. Eagerness to hear and know everything is no less fatal to solid piety, and cannot be too assiduously repressed. Through the ears, the soul finds itself occupied with any number of things, which afterwards distract and fill it, in spite of itself, even in the time of prayer. We should, therefore, choose some quiet place for our meditations, and especially for prayer, away from the tumult and noise of men. Curiosity, also, should be watched, otherwise it will lead to visits here and there, long and profitless conversations, indiscreet questionings, suspicions and conjectures, rash judgments, and endless conversations on public and private matters. In these things God is often offended, and they are incompatible with a spirit of prayer and true devotion.

Thus he who would embark on the interior life must renounce everything that excites his curiosity: all, that is, which affects the senses too vividly and conspires to agitate false excitements and dangerous passions. He should avoid concerning himself with the affairs of others, with public or private news, unless he is obliged to do so by virtue of his position or from personal interest. Not that one may not casually and occasionally see and hear such things, where there is no danger, but they should not be sought or desired or clung to, or their memory will loom too large in the mind.

Intellectual curiosity is equally dangerous, and if we would foster the habit of recollection we must learn to keep it within bounds. By intellectual curiosity I mean that immoderate desire to acquire knowledge, which causes people to study avidly the various sciences, and nearly always superficially. They devour every book as it comes out, more to show off than to improve their minds. I do not see how recollection can be compatible with such a disposition, which generally indicates a shallow mind.

Beware, then, of this defect. Or, if you are prone to it, do all you can to overcome it. Be content with such learning as is necessary to, or befits, your state. Confine your reading to such books, even religious ones, as are highly esteemed, and do not imitate those who flit from one book to another, and finish none. This is not the place to explain how such books should be read: I would merely state that in this matter one cannot guard oneself too carefully against idle curiosity.

There is another kind of temperament, which at first sight would seem to be favourable to recollection, but which is actually the reverse. It is that of persons of a romantic nature, whose imagination takes a firm hold of things and creates a happy hunting ground, based on memories of the past and dreams of the future. Such natures build castles in the air, complete with all due circumstance of person, place and action. These romantic imaginations enable their possessors to live in a state of great excitement, so much so that from their room they entertain the world. They love solitude, but for the wrong reason. They appear to be recollected, but are in fact merely preoccupied. They find the greatest difficulty in acquiring an habitual sense of the presence of God.

The practice of ejaculatory prayer is an excellent aid to recollection, because it tends to recall us often to ourselves and to God. It is a very good thing to form this habit, but we must be careful not to let it become a mere matter of routine. Such prayers must rise from the heart rather than from the lips, and are all the better when they consist of a simple turning of the soul towards God, unaccompanied by any words expressed or understood. We cannot take too much pains to acquire this method of prayer, and if by daily practice it becomes more frequent and grows into a habit, it will dispose the mind until we 'pray without ceasing' as the apostle commands us to do. [58]

Whether we are reading or meditating, or repeating vocal prayers, it is good to pause from time to time and let the soul quite suspend its own action to give place to the action of the Holy Spirit. If we feel at all touched by grace at such moments, we cannot do better than give way to it, and quietly rest in the feelings God gives us. When that impression has passed, we can resume our book or our prayers.

These transitory touches are but the beginning of infused prayer, and we ought to correspond to them with great fidelity. They are momentary visits, wherein God communicates Himself to the soul. Short though they are, they do us more good than any of the thoughts and affections of our own making. Why do we read or pray, except to attain to union with God? When, therefore, He comes and bestows on us a certain secret sense of His presence, we have what we desire. We should, therefore, yield to this sense as long as it lasts. It would be irreverent to go on with our previous occupation. By so doing, we would deprive ourselves of the effect of His visits, and cause them to be less frequent. St. Francis of Sales insisted very much on this point.

Passive recollection is not a passing visit from God, but an habitual sense of His presence in the soul. We feel that presence within us, and its effects are so deep and gracious that we feel no doubt that they can only come from God. The soul is filled and strengthened by an indefinable calm and peace, and a suspension of its natural powers, with which no natural pleasure of any kind is to be compared. It is not only in times of prayer that the soul experiences this peace, but in almost all it does. No matter what our occupation or company may be, we have only to enter into ourselves to experience God's presence in our soul as a faithful Friend.

And do not let those who have never experienced this peace, and cannot imagine it, pass it off as a fond dream. All the saints would rise up against them and tell them that they are wrong. And not only the saints, but all who follow the way of interior prayer. Nor is it a delusion of the devil. That could not be in the case of an habitual presence of God, in which imagination plays no part.

The chief effect of this prayer of recollection is to turn our vision inward, detaching us from external things and deadening their effect, so that, occupied with all that is passing within us, we cease to be moved by outward impressions. By that I do not mean what we are oblivious of them as happens in the case of ecstasy, where one is deprived of ordinary sensation. We feel, but we do not pause or reflect on the fact, since we are held by an inward delight more powerful than anything that could attract us from without. God thus withdraws the soul from communion with creatures, and binds it wholly to Himself, so that it feels itself alone with Him and pays no attention to anything else. This state of recollection is, properly speaking, the entrance to the interior life, and is the surest sign that a soul is in the passive state.

This presence is at first such as may be felt, because the sense of it is necessary in order to detach the soul from conversation with created things, and to inspire it with supreme contempt for the pleasure that is derivable from them. Once this effect is produced, the recollectedness leaves the surface of the soul and sinks deeper. The presence of God is no longer felt; we are merely aware of it, since for a time we retain the habit of reflecting on it. But at last we cease to perceive it, because, as we advance, we go out of ourselves and enter into God, and are less taken up with what passes within us.

As this habitual presence of God is the foundation of all the graces which He subsequently bestows on the soul, we cannot be too faithful in preserving it The love which the soul feels towards God in these early days leads it to constancy in prayer and to other devout exercises, to frequenting the sacraments and to the practice of bodily mortification. But good as these things are, we must pass further and withdraw altogether from created things, resorting to them only when absolutely necessary. As far as may be, we must put aside most of the good works which would draw us to external interests. For the one thing essential in this state is an entire yielding of oneself to God's action, and this requires retirement, silence, and withdrawal from all affairs except such as are called for by the duties of our state. These, needless to say, take precedence over everything else. Later on, we can resume these good works, and indeed add to them, when God gives the signal, and they no longer involve the risk of distracting the mind. Meanwhile, no liberty must be allowed to the senses, no curiosity indulged in, all idle thoughts must be rejected, and the heart kept free from all attachments. In a word, nothing must come between the soul and God.

Let it not be supposed that all this is necessarily painful. As long as sensible recollection persists, nothing is difficult. God asks of us what He wants in a manner so gracious and persuasive that it is almost impossible to refuse Him anything. We receive so many graces from Him that we feel that we shall never be able to do enough for Him in return. In short, we are in the first fervour of our love, and more than eager to prove our love to Him. The practices that, on account of their constant repetition, seem and are hard to one in the active way, are nothing to one in a state of passive recollection. Hours of prayer pass like minutes. The pleasures of the world cease to have any attraction, contacts with others that are unavoidable become wearisome, while one's friends that formerly seemed so delightful lose their charm. Even the demands of nature are yielded to with regret. What has brought about so remarkable a change? A faint foretaste of the joys of heaven. If this is the beginning of the spiritual life, what will be its consummation?

One word more. You want to be instructed concerning the things of God. You consult men, and thewritings of men; yet you do not apply to Him Who in one moment can give light to the humble soul, teaching it without sound of words, and imparting more in one single prayer of contemplation than could be obtained in years from the most spiritual of men. You weary your mind in order to be recollected in prayer, and no more is necessary than a good will and the use of such measures as shall prepare your soul aright. For it is absurd to expect to be recollected in time of prayer, if the mind is distracted at other times. You seek to make your prayer by your own efforts. God makes it within the soul so soon as, convinced of our powerlessness, we cease from action on our own part, and yield to His. He Himself calls us to this surrender, when He intends to act in us. You wish to enjoy peace, and you agitate and distress yourself to obtain it. You grieve at not feeling it, while you are doing everything that is calculated to drive it away. You forget that the God of peace dwells not in agitation nor in turmoil, but causes Himself to be felt like a soft wind [59], which is produced by and maintains a state of calm. You seek self when you think you are seeking God, and so you do not find Him.

Oh how astonished some persons would be if they knew how little labour is required for the attainment of simple recollection. But man is jealous of his own powers of action, and loves to attribute all things to himself. God is infinitely more jealous of His powers, and will have all attributed to Him. This is the cause of all the false ideas men have of the interior life, and of their poor attempts at it. God does nothing in anyone who fancies himself, and who wants to do everything. But He acts, well- pleased, in a soul that dwells quietly and humbly in His presence, drawing Him gently by its desires, expecting nothing from its own efforts, but all from His loving-kindness. In the moral world, as in the physical, God brings all things out of nothing. If only we will be humble and abase ourselves before Him, He will soon reveal His power.

57.   Ps. lxxxiii. 8.
58.   I Thess. v. 17
59.   Cf. 3 Kings xix. 12

Eleventh Maxim: A childlike spirit

Treat God as a child treats his Father.

It would seem that nothing should be easier or more common for Christians than to look upon God as their Father, and act towards Him with simplicity, confidence and abandonment. It is the very spirit of the New Law, and is what distinguishes it from the Old. One of the fundamental dogmas of our faith is that God the Father has adopted us in His Son Jesus Christ, and raised us up to the supernatural state of His children, whereby we are made heirs, indeed, of God and joint heirs with Christ; [60] an inheritance which gives us a right to heaven as our home and to the eternal possession of God. This title, child of God, presupposes and recalls to our minds the chief objects of our faith, is the foundation of our hope, and the paramount motive of our love.

Yet nothing is rarer among Christians than this filial disposition towards God; almost all are more inclined to fear than to love Him. They find it exceedingly difficult to have a complete trust in Him, to the extent of abandoning themselves totally to His divine Providence. What is so little known, and even less practised in the spiritual life and most difficult to human nature, is the casting of all our care upon Him, in the firm faith that nothing can be ordained by His Providence that will not work for our good, unless we ourselves place some obstacle in the way. [61]

This all comes from self-love which would persuade us that our interests are only safe so long as we have the control of them in our own hands. We cannot make up our minds to entrust them to God, and, in all that concerns us, to look upon Him as a Father, no matter how much our love is put to the test. We are ready to trust Him when He indulges us, sends us consolations and gives us all we ask. But when, to teach us to love and serve Him for His sake and not for our own, as such a Father deserves to be loved, He withdraws the comforts we have abused, refuses what would harm us, and offers us what is for our good but which we do not want, then we no longer think of Him as a Father but as a harsh task-master. His demands are distasteful to us and we are ready at any moment to quit His service. Even our spiritual director has the greatest difficulty to restrain us when he takes God's part against us.

Yet it is nevertheless true that God never shows Himself more truly a Father than in the trials He sends us. His crosses are the most precious favours He could bestow on us in this life, and the heavier the burden He lays upon those who have given themselves to Him, the more is it a proof of the love He bears them. Was not Our Lord the well-beloved Son, in Whom the Father was well pleased? [62] Yet how did He treat Him, from His birth to His last sigh upon the Cross? Was He less His Father when He gave Him up into the hands of wicked men; when to all appearances He forsook Him on the Cross, and suffered Him to die tortured and in shame? Surely not! And it may truly be said that if Calvary was the scene of Christ's love for His Father, it was no less the clearest demonstration of the Father's love for His Son. Judge by the consequences. All the glory and power and blessing which Our Lord possesses as man, He owes to the Cross. Did He not Himself say: Ought not Christ to have suffered these things, and so to enter into His glory? I His Father required that temporary proof of obedience at His hands, that He in turn might give Him an eternal proof of the magnificence of His reward.

With the example of Our Lord, then, before our eyes, never let us think that God is not acting as our Father when He asks sacrifices of us that are painful to nature; when, having asked and received our consent, He takes us at our word, and exacts the fulfilment of our promise. It is true that the Face He turns to us then may seem severe, and it is His justice rather than His love that we see; but never was He more our Father, never were the marks of His love more apparent to the eyes of faith.

Consider also the upbringing of a child. While weak and tender, he is nursed, carried, petted, indulged and soothed. But as he grows older, he is placed under a rule; he is obliged to do things which are unpleasant, and of which he does not as yet see the use. He is broken in to obedience and habituated to control his desires and follow the guidance of reason. When necessary, he is treated severely and chastised. Why? Solely in order to draw out his powers, to make a man of him, and to prepare him for a useful and happy life in the future, according to his state in life.

In the same manner does God act towards His children. He intends them for citizens of the heavenly Jerusalem. When they begin to give themselves up to Him, He makes the greatest allowances for their weakness. He lavishes sweetness and consolations upon them, in order to win their hearts. He makes all things easy to them. He removes temptations, pleases them and, as it were, makes Himself a child with them. But as they grow stronger and are capable of receiving solid lessons in the interior life, He adopts another plan. He attacks nature, pursues all its defects and vicious propensities, sparing none. He prescribes difficult duties, and requires their fulfilment with extreme severity. The language of grace is no longer tender and persuasive: it is strong, imperious, even threatening; the least resistance is rigourously punished. He proportions the exercises, the trials and temptations that He sends, to their strength and state. The more He has endowed them with powers natural and supernatural, the more He demands of them, until they are moulded to all the virtues, and have passed through all the degrees of holiness. When they have reached that point of perfection to which He desires to bring them, when they have become worthy of Him, then their spiritual education is complete, and He removes them to His kingdom, where He crowns their struggles and their obedience, making them everlastingly partakers of His glory and bliss.

Thus the interior life throughout its whole course is nothing other than an education divine and paternal, inspired and ruled by love. God, on His side, fulfils perfectly the role of a Father, Whose desire is to make us happy. Let us, then, on our part, do all He expects of us as His children.

Once again, let us take children as our pattern. What are the feelings that a well-disposed child entertains for his father? In the first place, great simplicity, ingenuousness and candour. A child has no notion of concealing or dissimulating with his father. He opens his heart to him, tells him all he feels, and that is how we should act towards God. In fear, joy or sorrow, we should go to Him with the candour and simplicity of children. He knows better than we do what is passing in us, but He likes us to speak to Him about it. He wants to be our confidant and friend. Do not be afraid, then, to address Him sometimes with loving reproaches: such holy liberty pleases Him; nothing displeases Him more than cold reserve.

The next thing noticeable in a child is his trust. Timid and distrustful where others are concerned, in his father he places unbounded confidence. He knows that his father loves him; that he cares for him, toils for him, plans for him, and has no other aim but his happiness. And so he neither cares nor troubles himself about his own welfare, but leaves all to his father, who provides for his wants, even for his innocent pleasures, forestalls his slightest wishes, and reads them in his eyes. He is persuaded that the advice, the lessons, the corrections of his father, the various tasks he imposes, the severity he uses towards him, even what seems to be hurtful, have no other object than his true happiness. He knows this, not by reasoning, but by instinct and experience.

If only we had the same confidence in our heavenly Father, Who is worthy of it infinitely more than any earthly father! If only we would make over to His Divine Providence the care of our spiritual interests; confide to His grace far more than to our own efforts our spiritual welfare and perfection. If only we were deeply convinced that God does all things and ordains all things for our good; that His precepts which act as a curb to our passions, the duties that seem so painful, the evils and afflictions He permits, the hidden dispositions by which He disturbs our plans and cuts across our undertakings, the very faults and falls He refuses to prevent in order that we may be humble and mistrust ourselves, are permitted solely with a view to our eternal good--if, I say, we believed these things, how God would be glorified by our trust, and what intimate care, what loving attentions would not our confidence draw down upon us.

St. Paul lays it down as an axiom of the spiritual life that all things--without exception -- work together unto good to them that love God. [63] What does loving God mean, save looking upon Him as a Father, speaking to Him, relying upon Him for everything, acting and cooperating with His grace, and, having done on our part all that He expects of us, trusting solely to His love and mercy? O filial trust! What anxiety you would spare Christians who sincerely desire their salvation, and how you would assure it much better than all the sufferings of mind that self-love brings in its train! Leave to your heavenly Father the direction of your inner life, follow quietly the attraction of grace, consult His holy will in all things, oppose it in nothing. For the rest, pay no heed to your foolish questionings, calm your imagination, and despise the vain fears that would weaken your trust in Him. This is the way to heaven, and if you meet with difficulties on the way, they come from you, not from God.

Obedience is another characteristic of a child's disposition: an obedience altogether founded on love, not arising from fear as is the servile obedience of slaves, nor dictated by a mercenary self- interest. An obedience which embraces without reserve its Father's will, not considering whether the carrying out of that will is easy or difficult, pleasant or otherwise. An obedience generous, prompt and courageous, neither complaining nor excusing itself, finding its reward in the joy of having done its duty in pleasing a Father it loves and respects. Is it thus that most Christians obey God? I doubt it: and why?

It is because for the most part they forget that God is their Father. They look upon Him in quite another light. Some fear damnation more than they desire their salvation. They are moved more by the thought of the pains of hell than by that of the joys of heaven. Fear is at the root of their obedience. They regard God as a harsh master, and a severe judge.

Now fear has the power to keep us from evil, but not to lead us to good. It is a curb, not a spur. It is the beginning, but only the beginning, of wisdom. [64] God does not mean us to stop there. From fear we ought to pass on to love; indeed, we are not fearing God when we only fear His chastisements, and we do not obey Him according to His will when we yield only to His warnings. So that this obedience is equally imperfect in its motive. It permits the whole weight of the yoke to be felt, but does not remove from the heart a secret longing to be rid of it. It limits itself to the letter of the law, and, as men naturally interpret the law in their own favour, its obligations are often imperfectly fulfilled

Others do, indeed, consider God as their rewarder. They serve Him from a motive of hope, but they care less for Himself than for the good things He promises. They hope, that is, for the possession of God, but less for His sake than for their own happiness. In other words, self is uppermost in their minds and they barely pay attention to anything else.

This motive is not bad, since it incites to well doing, but it is not pure enough, and if their obedience has no other stay, it will be weak and hesitating, and often fretful. True faith, which is evidenced by love, has very little influence on their conduct. The present good and evil counts with them as much as the good to come. And that is why they find it so difficult to practise virtue, which consists principally in mistrusting the pleasant things of this world, and accepting the unpleasant. We may indeed fear for them when certain temptations come upon them, which only the love of God can enable them to overcome.

It is not in fear, then, nor in self-interest, but in love that we
shall find the deep principle of the obedience which is due
to God, and nothing will inspire us with that love more than
the role of Father which God has deigned to assume for our
sakes. When, having meditated on this Name so tender and
on the dispositions it presupposes in God in my regard, I
consider that from all eternity He has loved me, not merely
as His creature but as His child; that He has gone so far as
to tell us in the Sacred Word that, even if a mother should
forget the child of her womb, yet will He never forget us;
[65] when I realize that He has raised us to be His sons by
adoption, [66] destined to be associated with His divine
Son in His heavenly inheritance and to share in His eternal
beatitude; when I consider, above all, the marvellous plan
of His paternal love and what it cost the Son to raise me to
that divine adoption, and the inestimable graces which
accompanied and have followed that amazing gift: what, I
say, can I refuse to such a Father, Whose only motive in all
He asks of me is the love He bears me, and the good He
wills to bestow upon me?

What can I see in His law but the loveliest and most just of
duties, namely to love Him; for in this consists the whole of
His law. [67] How can I regard this as a yoke or a burden?
Sweet, indeed, is His yoke and His burden light; [68] and
never will I regret having taken them upon me. My
endeavour, then, shall be to love this kindest of Fathers in
gratitude for His love for me; and to prove my love for Him
by an obedience which I shall regard as my greatest joy.
So, too, my greatest sorrow would be not to love Him, and
to disobey Him in the least thing.

Nor will I limit myself to the performance of those things
which He commands under pain of His displeasure. I shall
study to do what pleases Him. The least sign He gives me

shall be a law to me, and I will try to refuse Him nothing, complain of nothing, and submit with joy to all, even to the most painful dispensations of His Providence. For His name of Father always bids me look upon them as marks of His love, and trials of mine. Thus Job felt, when in the depth of his afflictions he cried: If we have received good things at the hand of God, why should we not receive evil? [69] And: Although He should kill me, yet will I trust Him. [70] And again: May this be my comfort, that afflicting me with sorrow, He spare not: nor I contradict the words of the Holy One. [71] So far should a Christian carry his confidence and submission towards such a Father.

How weak is human respect when it attacks a heart full of filial love. The attractions and seductions of the world do not interest the true child of God. He neither fears its threats nor its ridicule. He holds up his head and boldly declares his mind, when His Father's honour is at stake. If he hides himself from the sight of men, he does so through humility, never through weakness. He does nothing to draw attention to himself, and cares not whether he is seen or not seen, praised or blamed, esteemed or contemned. To him the world is as though it were not. In company or alone, his eyes are always fixed on his Father, and his concerns are with Him alone. How should he trouble himself about pleasing the world, when he does not wish to please even himself? He dreads nothing so much as having to think of himself; he does all he can to forget himself, and would shrink from diminishing his Father's glory by anything approaching self-complacency. And if by chance he should do so from time to time, he deeply regrets it as a real fault.

The delicacy of his love goes further still. Content to please God, he is in no way eager for his love to be recognized. He neglects nothing whereby he may be acceptable in

God's sight, but asks for no sign of assurance that he is so. He knows that self- love would rest satisfied with such an assurance, and his love for God would suffer accordingly.

60. Rom. viii. 17
61. Cf. Ps. liv. 23
62. Matt. iii. 17
63. Cf. Rom. viii. 28
64. Cf. Ecclus. I. 16
65. Cf. Isaias xlix. 15
66. Cf. Rom. xiii. 10
67. Cf Gal. iv. 5
68. Cf. Matt. xi. 30
69. Job. ii. 10
70. Job. xiii. 15
71. Job vi. 10

Twelfth Maxim: Fidelity

Beware of resisting the leadings of grace: be thoroughly generous in great things and in small.

It is proper to grace to strive against nature. Therefore, we must expect that it will frequently, or rather continually, demand of us such things as are contrary to our vicious or imperfect tendencies, and that consequently nature will offer a violent resistance, and will not yield until the last moment. The will, however, must always be on the side of grace. By the word 'will', I do not mean certain ineffective desires, certain repugnances or aversions which are not free, but a firm and determined resolution--not I would, but I will, triumphant equally over likes and dislikes.

Such a generous intention, firmly resolved to respond in everything to God's designs, is not often met with, even among those who think they have given themselves entirely to Him. At certain times of sensible fervour, we declare ourselves ready and willing for everything, and we fancy that our protestations spring from the depths of our will. But it is not so; they are only the effect of the glow of grace.

When that glow has abated and the soul is restored to itself and to ordinary grace, we are surprised to see that all our good intentions have vanished. Or else, like St. Peter, we presume on our strength and, so long as danger is afar off, we fancy ourselves ready to confront everything. But when the opportunity presents itself we yield, as the apostle did, to the slightest temptation. There is a great difference, said a holy man who spoke from experience, between sacrificing one's life to God in a transport of fervour, and doing the same thing at the foot of the gallows. The true disposition of the will is to be judged at the actual moment of the sacrifice, when the temporary effect of the heavenly warmth is withdrawn, and the soul has cooled down and returned to a state of ordinary grace.

Therefore we ought not lightly to imagine that we have this good will: rather we should always fear that we have it not. We are not, indeed, to be pusillanimous, but we are bound to mistrust ourselves always and rely solely on help from heaven, confident that it will never fail us in time of need. We are so weak that we cannot be sure of victory beforehand. The slightest presumption renders us unworthy of it, and often the enemy snatches the victory from our hands, just when we think it is ours.

Do you want to be sure of never resisting God? Then remember always Our Lord's own words: The spirit indeed is willing, but the flesh is weak. [72] We must watch and pray, as He bids us, that we enter not into temptation. Watch, so as not to expose ourselves or give advantage to the enemy; pray, in order that we may obtain from God the strength we need. Abiding, thus, in the salutary fear of being unfaithful to grace, God will preserve us from all evil. Or, if He permits us from time to time to realize our weakness, it will never be by a deadly fall: He will interpose His own hand between us and the blow, to prevent it from doing us harm. He will quickly raise us up again, and we shall be all the stronger afterwards.

The fear of resisting grace may be looked upon in yet another light. Such resistance is the greatest evil we have to dread. When God intends to take possession of a soul and direct it himself He gives it much instruction relative to its perfection. He watches with extreme care over its thoughts, words, acts and motives. He overlooks nothing, examines every action, and keenly rebukes the slightest unfaithfulness.

Now the soul cannot be too attentive to the light it thus receives from God, and His secret reproaches: it is of the greatest importance to pay them every regard. For in the first place, if we resist God's will, we at once arrest the progress of our own perfection. We place a stumbling-block in our own way, and make no advance until we have surmounted it. Not only shall we not advance, but we shall fall back; for it is an axiom of the spiritual life that we must either go forward or fall back. In the second place, one grace rightly used attracts a second, the second brings a third, and so on, for graces are linked together; they form a chain which ends in holiness and final perseverance. In the same way, a grace rejected deprives us of the next, and therefore of those which should follow. And this may be carried so far as to prove fatal in the long run.

Therefore it is always extremely dangerous to break this chain, and as it is certain that we shall undoubtedly arrive at that perfection that God expects of us if we advance faithfully from grace to grace, so it is equally certain that we run a grave risk in the matter of our salvation if we break the chain of graces in any way whatsoever.

This is especially true of certain principal graces which form, as it were, the master links in the chain, upon which so much depends. Such are the grace of one's vocation, an attraction to interior prayer, and others of like nature. They are a kind of starting point from which God is going to lead us to our final haven. If we respond faithfully and assiduously, we will have nothing to fear, but if we reject His overtures at the outset we can never be sure of having a second opportunity.

But I should warn timid souls that the chain is not broken by faults of inadvertence and impulse or even of imprudence and indiscretion: in other words, by sins of frailty. It is only broken by sins knowingly, wilfully and repeatedly committed. For God does not leave us just for one fault; He returns again and again, and is as patient as the end He has in view is great. Even when He sees that we are determined to have nothing to do with Him, He does not withdraw altogether.

He acts in a similar manner when He is asking certain sacrifices of us. Sometimes He pursues a soul for years before He wearies, especially if the sacrifice is important and the soul feels a great repugnance for it. The moment when His pursuit ceases is known to Him alone. Should the soul want to withdraw itself from the order of supernatural Providence, it is to be feared that it may never re-enter it, and even its eternal salvation may be endangered. God showed St. Teresa the place she would have had in hell, had she lost that which was prepared for her in heaven. For her there was no middle course, it was one thing or the other; and there are many souls in a like state without knowing it.

This is one of the principal reasons why masters of the spiritual life so strongly urge the duty of recollectedness and correspondence with grace. The soul cannot attend too carefully to the warnings that God does not cease to give, constraining it to do good and avoid evil. The soul should observe the greatest fidelity in following these inspirations of grace. This attention and docility Our Lord Himself made the distinctive marks of His disciples: My sheep, He said, follow Me, because they know My voice. [73] And it may be affirmed that the whole system of true direction consists in moulding souls to such a disposition.

Finally, we ought to question God's will in nothing, great or small. It is not our place to decide on the greater or less importance of the things God requires of us, and we can so easily fall into error on such points. Besides, if God signifies His will concerning any matter, however small, that intimation at once invests it with importance, and, more than all else, we are bound to consider the intention and good pleasure of so great a Master. What, in itself, was the eating or abstaining from a certain fruit? And yet the happiness of the human race depended upon the observance of so apparently trifling a command. God is the absolute arbiter ofthe graces He bestows upon us, and also of the conditions He attaches to them. On our fidelity in a seemingly trivial matter may depend many graces which He has in store for us.

Opportunities for doing great things for God are rare, but those for doing little things for Him are continually arising, and it is precisely in these little things that the refinement of love shows itself. Nothing proves the depth of our love for God and our desire to please Him more than the conviction that nothing is little where His service is concerned. And how, indeed, can we expect to be faithful to Him in big things if we are careless in obeying Him in small? It is just these that are more within our reach and more adapted to our weakness. The bigger things, on the other hand, call for great efforts, which are often beyond our strength, and of which it would be presumptuous to deem ourselves capable. Great acts of virtue are God's work rather than ours, and if the smaller ones seem to belong to us, none the less God's action plays the greater part in them also.
Our fidelity, then, is not perfect unless it embraces everything, without exception. We ought to judge of the service due to God by that which we ourselves expect of

others. We look for exactness, promptness, and thoroughness, and would be offended if our orders were not carried out, just because they were not gravely important. Is it too much, then, to serve God as we desire to be served ourselves?

Faithfulness in little things keeps us humble, and shields us from vanity, and is of inestimable value in God's sight if it proceeds from a high motive. By it we acquire that extreme purity of conscience which brings us very close to God. The special characteristic of His own holiness was precisely His utter incompatibility with the least stain of sin. So it is with the saints, allowing for due proportion in the comparison.

How mistaken are those souls who try to keep anything back from God. Who, so to speak, bargain with Him, who consent to give Him certain things but obstinately refuse Him others; who keep a watch on themselves in certain directions but are negligent in others; who set bounds to their perfection and say within themselves: I will go so far and no farther. Can they not see that the very thing that they withhold from God is just what He is particularly asking of them, and of which He reproaches them so frequently and insistently? If He presses His demand, it is not for His sake but for ours. Not only does He see more clearly than we do, but He alone knows what is best for us, indeed what is necessary for our advancement. And His very insistence is a sure sign that what He asks is more important than we think.

Here, then, is a subject for our examination of conscience. We must overlook nothing, spare nothing, search the innermost corners of our heart, lest there be some hidden reservation, some rapine in the holocaust. And, having made a thorough search, let us beg God to bring His own light to bear on the dark corners of our soul, making our interior dispositions clear to us, constraining us to refuse Him nothing, and using all His authority to take from us what we have not the courage to give Him.

72.   Matt. xxvi . 41
73.   Cf. John x. 4

Thirteenth Maxim: Mortification

Never cease to struggle with the enemy that lives within the soul.

What is that old man that St. Paul bids us crucify, and which Christ in His own person bound to the Tree of the Cross, to teach us what it deserves and how we must treat it? It is the flesh or, in other words, it is everything within us that is opposed to the spirit of God. This is the meaning of the apostle who, under the name of the flesh, comprised those vices which have the body for their object, as well as those which originate in the mind. All the former pertain to sensuality, the latter to pride or inordinate self-esteem.

In order to understand the real nature of the war with themselves to which all Christians are bound, and of their two natures, spiritual and animal, whose inclinations are so diametrically opposed to each other and tend to their mutual destruction, we must go right back to original sin and to the two great wounds it inflicted on us. Only thus shall we obtain a true conception of Christian mortification, of its necessity, its extent and continuity.

When Adam came from the hands of the Creator, his spirit was humble and subject to God, his body obedient and subject to the spirit. Everything within was in order, and all he had to do was to remain in that state. Sin destroyed that order, when Adam rebelled against God. His revolt arose from a principle of pride, and in an absurd hope of becoming like God by eating the forbidden fruit. The rebellion of his flesh was meant to humble his pride by making him realize that anyone who, abusing his reason, aspires to equality with God, deserves as a punishment to be reduced to the level of the beast, and subject like them to the empire of the senses.

Therefore, the first thing he perceived after his sin was this rebellion of the flesh. It was the indubitable sign and witness of his degradation, and, had he not been blinded by sin, that disorder, which he was ashamed to look upon, would have taught him how much more disgraceful and odious was the rebellion of his spirit against God. God had to open his eyes and enable him to judge of the exceeding disorder of his spirit by the shame which he felt in consequence of the disorder of his flesh.

We, unhappy children of Adam, are all born with a fatal tendency to this twofold disorder. The flesh disobeys the spirit, its appetites and motions forestall the will. The will is only too ready, first to consent, then to excite the appetites and finally to become their slave. Reason has the power to regulate the necessary appetites, such as eating and drinking, and should have absolute command over the rest. But it is weak enough to give way to them, and not only gratifies them, frequently beyond necessity and contrary to the Creator's will, but degrades itself so low as to seek only the pleasure attached to the satisfaction of the senses, resting therein as in its final end, using its ingenuity and powers to procure refined voluptuousness of every kind, even to the over-stepping of the immutable bounds of nature, and yielding to excesses which nature itself abhors. It is a most humiliating state of affairs, which degrades man much lower than the beasts, and which yet he feels so little that he counts it a merit and a glory.

The disobedience of the spirit towards God goes, if possible, further still. We affect an absolute independence. We consider our liberty to consist in doing whatever we please, without exception, and we look on this unlimited liberty as a right which cannot be justly disputed. We are annoyed by the dominion God exercises over us, necessary, mild and moderate though it be, and favourable to our present well-being, and having no other end in view than our eternal happiness. Lawful, reasonable and wise as it is, we are continually trying to shake off, or at least to weaken, His yoke. Every law He lays down for us seems a blow aimed at our rights; every commandment a burden to us, every prohibition a source of irritation. It only requires for a thing to be forbidden us to make us want it all the more. This strange disposition, which every one will find in himself if he will take the trouble to look deep enough, arises from a collosal pride which recognizes no master, a mad idea of our own excellence, and an utter blindness to all that concerns our own good.

These are the disorders that the Gospel would have us recognize, and teaches us to cure. The whole of the Christian moral law is nothing else than a remedy for these two fundamental disorders, and for that purpose proposes for our use two kinds of mortification, as reasonable as they are indispensable. The aim of the first is to subjugate the body to the mind; that of the second to submit the mind to God, and so restore the original order in which man was created, and repair the evil caused by sin. These two methods are called respectively exterior and interior.

The first stage in exterior mortification, which is absolutely binding on all Christians, is to abstain from all pleasures forbidden by the divine law; to observe moderation in the use of those that are lawful, using them not as ends in themselves, but as means, as the Creator intended them to be used, and generally to observe the precepts of the Church.

The second stage goes further. It refuses all unnecessary indulgence to the senses. It allows food only to hunger, drink to thirst, sleep to fatigue, clothes and shelter to necessity, suffering nothing to gratify taste or encourage effeminacy. All excessive pampering of the body foments its rebellion against the spirit, and we know only too well from experience that it is always ready to abuse anything in the way of excess. A mortified Christian leads an ordinary life, in no way singular but simple, sober and even, and strictly according to the rules of temperance and moderation. He looks upon his body as a bad servant that grudgingly obeys, and is always endeavouring to throw off the yoke. That is why he keeps it in strict dependence, and so subjects it to the spirit that not only does it not hinder but it actually assists the spirit's operations. Such is the divine law, as reason alone tells us. The Gospel does no more than urge its observance and help us to carry it out.

The advantage of this moderate but steady mortification is that it allows no room for pride, is hardly noticed, and shields us from the excesses of an indiscreet fervour. Moreover, the flesh is already sufficiently subdued when it finds itself reduced to the bare necessities, and deprived of all that is superfluous.

However (and this is the third degree of mortification), God sometimes inspires pious souls to perform voluntary penances. These may be necessary, either for the expiation of sin, for the subduing of pride, or to help in resisting violent temptations. Nothing of this nature, however, should be undertaken without the advice of a confessor, and even the confessor should act in such cases with the utmost discretion.

Because we read in the lives of some saints that they practised extraordinary austerities, our imagination is forthwith fired, and we set out to imitate them, thinking that we cannot grow holy otherwise, and that then we shall infallibly do so. In this we are doubly mistaken, for unless God asks these austerities of us they are not necessary to our sanctity; and, indeed, unless inspired and directed by grace, may take away from instead of adding to it. We may admire the acts of the saints, humble ourselves because we have neither their courage nor their love of God, and be ashamed that we do so little in comparison with them. But to copy them in this particular respect is unwise in the extreme, unless God makes known to us (as He did to them) His will concerning it, and until that will is confirmed by the one who stands in God's place to us.

Mortification of the spirit brings the flesh into subjection much more efficaciously than any bodily austerity, for obvious reasons. The rebellion of the flesh against the spirit is, as I said before, the consequence and punishment of the rebellion of the spirit against God. Therefore, when we bring all our strength to bear on subjecting our spirit to God, we immediately attack the principle of the body's disorder. And God, seeing that the spirit is in submission to Him, causes the trouble due to its pride to cease, and Himself reduces the flesh to a state of obedience. The more humble we are, the less exposed shall we be to rebellion on the part of the flesh.

That is why interior mortification is incomparably more necessary, because it goes to the root and source of the trouble. But what are we to mortify in the soul? Everything, without exception. Sin has infected with its poison the passions, the mind, the will, even the very depth of the soul. Such is the war of man against himself, of grace against nature. And in this war, we may never lay down our arms, for so long as we live the enemy is never wholly overcome. Cast down he may be, but the slightest negligence on our part will cause him to rise up again.

Let us begin with the passions. In themselves, they are not evil: they are only a quick movement of the soul by which it tends to seek good and repel evil. Such they were in the beginning, and so God intended them to be. But since the Fall, the soul does not know its true good, nor its real evil. It no longer looks on these things from God's point of view, but from its own. It calls that good which flatters its pride and self-love, all that procures it some passing pleasure. And it calls that evil which humiliates and thwarts it, and disturbs the repose it finds, not in God but in created things. The passions, now the offspring of a blind will, and guided by a reason which no longer sees clearly, are thus mistaken in their object, which they proceed to pursue with excessive ardour. And because its falsity renders it unsatisfying, their craving increases in proportion. Always dissatisfied, they continue to seek an ever elusive happiness. Disappointed in one object, they turn blindly to another of the same kind, only to find themselves as starved as before. And so, unless it is enlightened by the light of grace, the soul continues in its error, until death puts an end to all deception.

Thus the primary duty of a Christian is to deprive the passions of all that feeds them, to check their impetuosity, quench their ardour, and prevent even their first emotions. To this end he must bring under control the senses which suggest to the passions their object. He must bridle the imagination which depicts it in seductive colours and thus kindles desire, and he must keep a curb on every inordinate inclination. It is not enough to forbid indulgence in what is manifestly sinful: those things must be cut off which are dangerous and doubtful or in any way apparently evil. The passions must even be deprived of things which are lawful and innocent in themselves, as soon as there is a danger of one's becoming too attached to them, since all inordinate attachment is liable to be harmful.

But such a war is not ended in a day. It must be waged remorselessly. There can be no question of any truce or peace, where such dangerous enemies are concerned. At times, the passions will appear to be dead, but they are only lulled. They revive as soon as our vigilance relaxes, and they rekindle in the heart a new conflagration, much more difficult to extinguish. Nor must we confine ourselves to the passions: we must attack also those affections which are purely natural; inclinations, repugnances, everything that fet- ters the heart and prevents it from being utterly free. Much more is involved than we think, once we are determined to know ourselves thoroughly, and to con- tend against every single thing within us that opposes the kingdom of grace. For grace purposes nothing less than the death of the purely natural spirit, in order that it may be reborn in the supernatural order. All men must act by reason, but the Christian must go further and be guided by a supernatural principle. St. Paul even applied this to our ordinary animal actions. Whatever you do, he says, whether you eat or drink, do all to the glory of God. [74] You can judge by this how far we must carry our interior mortification.

It is not enough to stop at our natural affections. We must not spare our sensitiveness, that excessive touchiness which reduces us to tears at the slightest word or the least contradiction, at the mere appearance, I do not say of contempt but of inattention or indifference or coolness on the part of others. There are very few Christians who have brought their sensitiveness completely under control, who in the course of their ordinary day ask for nothing, take exception to nothing and are indifferent to praise or blame. Alas! people complain, and not without reason, that pious folk are actually more sensitive, more difficult to get on with, take umbrage more quickly, than others. Do not give cause for this reproach, both for your own sake and for the honour of religion. Extreme sensitiveness is an unfailing source of distress. Our peace of mind is destroyed, we become suspicious of our neighbours, we look upon everything with a jaundiced eye, charity is lessened, and we run the risk of giving a fatal form to our feeling of resentment.

And that is not all. Even in the good you have in view, moderate the vivacity of your impulses, your eagerness, your activity. Try to keep yourself always in hand, [75] rise superior to your impatience, do not stop merely at its external signs but stifle its hidden movements as soon as they arise, and the moment you perceive them prevent them from gaining the least sway over you. The complete possession of oneself, which is the work of grace, is one of the greatest blessings in life; it makes for inward peace, spiritual joy, and evenness of soul. It edifies and wins over our neighbour, dries up the source of many faults, and leaves us the free exercise of all our powers to perceive and perform successive duties as they present themselves.

So much for the passions. As regards the mind, how many things there are to be mortified! From the first dawn of reason, the mind is filled with prejudices contrary to the Gospel in all that concerns honour, riches, pleasures and the habits of the world. Who does not regard high birth as something desirable, which raises one above one's neighbours, and yet what is it in God's sight? It is nothing. What is it according to the standard of the Gospel? An obstacle to humility. Until our mind on this point is the mind of Christ, [76] we cannot call ourselves His disciples. Again, who is not ashamed of low birth, and sensitive to the thoughts and remarks of others on the subject? Reason tells us that this is folly, but will never convince us. As against these ideas, the Gospel sets before us Our Lord's own choice. He appeared on earth in the lowliest of conditions, and though due to be born of the seed of David, the man after God's own heart, waited until the royal family had sunk so low that an artisan was counted for His father. Yet how hard we find it to conform our mind in this respect to the mind of Christ.

Some, of course, are called to fill high positions in Church and State, but power of this kind should always be feared rather than coveted. Yet many hanker after the authority that power brings, instead of dreading it as the Gospel bids. They are loath to obey but quick to command, slow to serve but eager to be served. It is the same with regard to poverty and wealth. The rich esteem themselves superior to the poor, and yet Our Lord chose poverty for Himself, and showed a special love for the poor. Indeed, we are told that He had not where to lay His head. [77] And yet how quick we are to prefer a life of ease and comfort to one of toil and suffering.

Was it thus that the early Christians lived? Did they not rather dwell together as brethren, having but one heart and one mind, holding their love feasts together, with honour, as St. Paul says, preferring one another. [78] What an immense forest of preconceptions must be hewn down before we attain to the literal practice of the Christian moral law, or can hope to see things in the same light as Our Lord views them.

But it is not enough merely to demolish these prejudices, we must strike at the root which is within ourselves. It is there that mortification must bring its fire and sword! Where will you find the man who does not esteem himself above his deserts; who does not presume on his gifts and talents, and rely on his own judgments? Who is not envious of the success of others professing the same calling, unwilling that they should be preferred to himself? Who does not dread the shadow of contempt more than death, and is not acutely sensitive to the slightest whisper against his good name?

Is this the mind of Jesus? Did He not in all His teaching and by His example preach humility, contempt and hatred of oneself? Did He not will to be despised and rejected of men, to be crushed like a worm of the earth, to suffer humiliations, scorn and infamy, even to the shameful death of the Cross? [79] He suffered the sacrifice of His reputation, and yet, according to our notions, how necessary it was for Him to preserve it, seeing that He came to be the Lawgiver, the Example, the Saviour of mankind. But it was by that sacrifice that man was saved. How then can we think highly of ourselves, believe in our own worth, strive to raise ourselves in the good opinion of others, or deceive ourselves so far as to believe that the preservation of our reputation is necessary for the glory of God? Shall we never think upon the truth that what Our Lord was He was in our stead, to teach us what we should be?

Now do you begin to perceive the full extent to which interior mortification must reach, and the series of long and

painful struggles to which we are committed if we would
be like our divine Master? Be not weary of learning your
duties, nor terrified at their number and difficulty; grace is
all-powerful and by its aid you will reach your goal.

It is against the will that the heaviest blows must be dealt.
This is the dominant faculty of the soul and the most
corrupt, for in it sin takes its rise and attains its growth. The
understanding is often enlightened and convinced, while
the will resists and refuses to surrender. Attack it then, and
determine on curbing its intractability. Deal with it so that
it may grow yielding and obedient to God and to man. On
no account allow it the freedom of which it is so jealous,
but bend it with all your strength to the dispositions of
Divine Providence, and to the will of others. Allow it no
choice, accustom it to be indifferent, and let its rule be
cheerfully to accept all vicissitudes great or small as they
arise.

The will must die to its own likes and dislikes. It must
resist its inclinations and do violence to its aversions. It
must study to go against itself in all things, and to repress
its own desires. It must be willing to see its hopes
disappointed, its schemes brought to naught, its projects
laid on one side or resisted. It must allow itself no self-
interest, and must consider itself in nothing. It may enjoy
divine consolations, but it must not depend upon them, and
must be content to see them withdrawn without regret. It
must receive crosses, and all manner of crosses, at first
uncomplainingly, then submissively, and finally with joy. It
must go so far as to desire never to be separated from the
cross, nor by so much as a single word to take any steps to
be freed from it. It must rest in the hands of God, and of
those who represent Him, as wax receives the figure
impressed upon it, or as water, having no form of its own,

assumes that of the vessel in which it is placed. Its life, its
movement, its activity must exist solely for the glory and
good pleasure of God.

O death of the will, how difficult and rare it is! What
Christian, nay what saint, exists who seeks nothing in and
for himself? That is the height of perfection, but few there
are who attain it; indeed, who even profess to desire it.

The value of this death is in proportion to its difficulty and
rarity. What an inestimable advantage it is to be raised
above all the events and happenings of life, above health
and sickness, riches and poverty, esteem and contempt,
honours and humiliations, good report and evil; above
natural friendship or aversion, above all attachment, all
inclination, all repugnance: amid all the ups and downs of
the spiritual life, in consolation or trials, to cling solely to
the will of God; loving, trusting and resting in it alone, and
partaking thus of its sanctity and changelessness.

I will say nothing of what I have called the mortification of
the real depths of the soul. This is beyond our scope, and
indeed beyond that of ordinary grace. It is the work of God
alone, and is reserved solely for those whom He proposes
to bring through the terrible trials that lead to this death.
Such is the lot of very few, and those who are not called to
it would attempt in vain to understand its nature.

Have I opened a sufficiently wide field for the Christian
combat? Have I given some idea of the relentless war to be
waged against self? Of the courage, patience and endurance
necessary in order to enter upon it, persevere in it, and
arrive at a full and final victory? Do you now realise what
that old man is, on whose fall the new man is to rise? Have
I with good reason shown you that he is the cause of all our

miseries, of all our misfortunes, now and to come? One thing is certain: whether we undertake this spiritual combat or no, he will cost us many a tear.

74.   I Cor. x. 31
75.   Cf. Ps. cxviii. 109
76.   Cf. Phil. ii. 5
77.   Matt. viii. 20
78.   Rom. xii. 10
79.   Cf. Phil. ii. 8

Fourteenth Maxim: Contemplative prayer

When God bids you be still in prayer, humble yourself silently before His Majesty.

It is well known that there are two kinds of mental prayer: meditation and contemplation. Meditation is to contemplation what active recollection is to passive. In meditation, all the powers of the soul, the memory, understanding and will, and even the imagination, have full scope, and from each is drawn what is most suitable to the end in view. A distinct subject is presented before the mind, on which reflections are made, and affections and resolutions formed. There are many good books on the subject, and I shall say little here respecting it.

In contemplation, or prayer properly so called, the soul neither reflects nor forms affections and resolutions. Yet neither are the understanding and will idle. For if the contemplation be distinct, the understanding sees, though without reasoning, the object presented to it by God. If it be confused, and offers to the soul no special object, the understanding holds itself in the presence of God, humbles itself before His supreme Majesty, and listens silently to the instruction given without sound or distinctness of words (which is the manner in which God's instruction is usually given). This attention is itself an act of the understanding, unperceived because so simple, but not therefore less real. The confused, general and indistinct object, which is then presented to the soul, is God Himself, but hidden in a cloud of faith; whereas in distinct contemplation, God unfolds one of His perfections or some particular mystery of religion.

We may form some idea of these two kinds of contemplation, if we remember the different ways in which we look at things about us, sometimes fixing our eyes on a certain point, at other times regarding vaguely without noticing anything in particular.

Nor is the repose of the will in contemplation to be considered as inaction. In the first place, its freedom is being continually exercised, since we are at prayer because we choose to be so, and frequently have to resist the temptation to give it up on account of distractions, dryness, or even evil thoughts which assail us at such times. Secondly, the will is either in a state of union, or in a constant tendency to union, with God, since it is only with that purpose that it perseveres in this kind of prayer. In the third place, it receives a sense of divine sweetness which gives place to joy and peace. Lastly, if the soul experiences nothing, and the time of prayer is spent in suffering, the will is then in a state of sacrifice, which it accepts in submission to God's good pleasure. Moreover, in that true repose which God bestows on the soul, as in the false repose which is the result of delusion, there is always some action on the part of the understanding and will.

The difference between the real and false repose is, not that the soul acts in true prayer and is silent in false, but that in the former God is the agent, whereas the second is due either to the imagination or the devil. However it may be-- and I do not wish to press the matter here--it would be wrong to call the holy repose in which God holds the soul during contemplation idleness, and no one should feel obliged to give it up on that account. But what one should do is this. One should examine by the rules laid down by the saints whether or not this repose comes from God. If it does, who would be rash enough to dare to disturb the peace of a soul in which God's action is taking place? If it does not, then the soul must be undeceived and set right.

These rules are as follows. In the first place, so long as we have the free use of our powers and can meditate with ease, we ought not to leave off. But it is the advice of spiritual writers that when we have sufficiently absorbed the truths we have been meditating on, and have considered them under every aspect, we should either wholly or in part cease from acts of the understanding and pass on to those of the will, which are much more essential, and lead us to love the truths we have already learned. For the aim of meditation is to move the will, and rouse it to shun vice and practise virtue.

Secondly, after meditation has been practised for some time, and the proper fruit has been derived therefrom, one begins to be aware that God is drawing the will to a particular state of rest. The will now produces no distinct affections or, if it wants to do so through long habit, it is gently checked and drawn to enjoy rather than to act. It is then that the soul is entering into the passive way. God Himself is leading it, and it would be harmful to the soul's advancement if it offered any resistance.

Thirdly, it is sometimes the case that a person truly devoted to God finds his efforts to meditate all in vain. If, after many attempts to do so, he finds himself unable to succeed, whether by reason of the simplicity of his mind which takes things in at a glance, or because of the bouyancy and vivacity of his imagination, or from any other cause, he would do well, on the advice of his confessor, to try simply to remain quiet in the presence of God, entreating the Holy Spirit to teach him to pray; or, like Samuel and David, listening to whatever God has to say to him in his heart. If this method suits him, if he feels calm and at peace, and comes away from such times of prayer more devoted to God's service and more determined to overcome himself, then he may take it that his prayer is good, and that God is acting in it. The effects will be the guarantee, and these are always peace, spiritual joy, the love of God, and an effectual desire to advance in virtue, which are always the fruits of the Holy Spirit. [80]

Fourthly, it may occur that when we betake ourselves to prayer, we feel the powers of the soul fettered, so that we cannot bring them to bear on the subject on which we proposed to meditate. For instance, we take up a book such as the Imitation, or one of similar character, but we have no sooner laid it down that we lose all recollection of what he have been reading, and the mind remains as it were in a vacuum. Now if this inability to think is accompanied by a sweet peace, which fully occupies the soul, it is one of the most assured signs that God is placing the soul in a state of passive prayer, and we must beware of making any effort to withdraw from that way. Even if this inability to meditate is accompanied by perplexity, darkness and temptation, yet if the soul is true and stands firm against these storms, they will soon pass and be followed by a great calm, and may be regarded as a preparation for the most signal favours of God.

In the last place, the usual proof that our prayer is good is the generous and continued practice of interior mortification. There is no cause for apprehension concerning the prayer of a person who is single hearted, straightforward, docile, humble, capable of great self-control, endowed with good will, ready to undertake cheerfully all the means suggested to it for overcoming faults, acknowledging them frankly and taking rebukes all in good part. If the spirit of God guides the rest of his conduct, we can hardly imagine that it will forsake him in the time of prayer.

But the application of these rules is a matter for the director. We should not judge ourselves, else we shall run the risk of deceiving ourselves. Humility and obedience are the two cardinal points on which the interior life turns. Therefore, when we believe it to be God's will that we should leave the ordinary way, we should in all simplicity represent our state to our spiritual guide, and thus enable him to decide. This is all the more necessary, since without his advice we cannot maintain ourselves in the different states of prayer. We ought also to keep him informed of all that takes place in our souls, in order that he may shield us from delusion, and strengthen us against temptations and trials.If, through lack of knowledge or prejudice against contemplative prayer, the director should mistakenly decide regarding our state, we must at once acquiesce in his decision, and do as he wishes. Thus St. Teresa abstained for a whole year from contemplative prayer by order of her confessor. Nevertheless, should we feel a certain discomfort, an inward constraint, which seems to us a sure sign that the director was taking us out of our proper sphere and making us go against God's action, then we might consult other confessors more enlightened and follow their advice. Thus St. Teresa, condemned as we have said by the doctors of Alcala, was reassured by St. Peter of Alcantara and St. Francis Borgia. God always blesses obedience and submission of the judgment. He will either, in His own way, cause the confessor to see our state in its true light, or else direct us to some other person.

I have said that God alone can, and may, bid the reason be silent in time of prayer. He has endowed the soul with powers, in order that they may be used so long as He grants them liberty. It was the false and heretical doctrine of Molinos that man ought to annihilate them himself: that is to say, reduce them to inaction. But any such inaction, voluntarily produced, would render us a prey to every freak of the imagination and every delusion of the heart.

Besides, according to the principles of true philosophy, the soul cannot of itself fetter its powers. This requires a superior agent, distinct from itself, and acting upon it with irresistible force. When God binds the soul in this way, it is amazed by the power brought to bear upon it, and perceives clearly that it comes from without. Sometimes it attempts with all its own strength to resist it, but all to no purpose. Anyone who knows this state and speaks of it, will tell you that one can do nothing: neither use one's memory, make any reflection, or excite any emotion. I am become as a beast (of burden) before Thee [81] says the Psalmist, and that is perfectly true; we become like a log of wood, waiting for God to kindle it.

These are the usual expressions on the part of persons who have experienced this state. They do not place themselves in it, for that would be a contradiction. Moreover, when sensible tokens of grace are withdrawn, which frequently happens, this state is far from giving pleasure to the soul; it is, on the contrary, very painful, being absolutely contrary to nature. We can only continue in this condition by sheer fidelity, because we cannot doubt that it is God's will. If we listened to our own promptings, we should renounce it altogether.

A confessor who is not on his guard may be deceived, and may lend an ear to the description of fictitious states of the soul. But if he knows what contemplation is, and if nothing is kept back from him, he cannot possibly confound real inability to pray with that state of inaction for which one is oneself responsible.

Let it not be supposed that true contemplation is an act which, being once entered upon, continues naturally and needs no renewal. This error, if taught by any mystic, lapses into the heresy of Molinos. I say, if taught, for it may well have happened that those who opposed it were mistaken, and took for contemplation the act by which the soul gives itself to God, and consecrates itself to His service in order to fulfil His will in all things. This latter act has no need of renewal, so long as we are faithful and do not go back on it, for it always subsists in intention and in fact. That does not mean to say that it is a continuous act, which is never suspended nor interrupted. It is an act, transitory in itself but abiding in its effects, so long as it not annulled by a contrary act. It is as though I formed the intention of making a journey and set out on the road. There is no need for me to be continually renewing my intention: I just carry on towards my journey's end, without stopping on the way or turning aside from it.

80.   Cf Gal. v. 22
81.   Ps. lxxii. 23

Fifteenth Maxim: Difficulties in prayer

Cling not to sensible sweetness: suffer dryness with a good heart.

This maxim refers to contemplative prayer, and to the manner in which those who practise it should act. As a rule, in the beginning, this kind of prayer is most attractive. God gives the soul a certain consciousness of His presence. [82] Having introduced it into His banqueting hall, He inundates it with favours. Here is a paradise of delights of which it had no conception. Here it breathes a different atmosphere, and delights in a liberty hitherto unknown; the heart is too narrow to contain the blessings lavished on it. But when it feels itself abandoned, sighs and tears are intermingled with exclamations of joy. This state may last some time. The Bridegroom does, indeed, hide Himself from time to time, but only so that the soul may long for Him more intensely. Then the soul hastens to recall Him, seeks Him anxiously, and derives fresh comfort when He returns.

In thus giving it a foretaste of those pure and deep joys of which He is the source, God intends the soul to feel an aversion and contempt for the false pleasures incident to the enjoyment of created things. Experience is a better teacher than theory, for the latter only appeals to the mind. But what happens then? The wretched self-love which we all have within us makes ill use of God's favours. Hardly has it tasted them than it seeks them eagerly, gloats over them with a complacency which it refuses to acknowledge, and persuades the soul to make them the motive and end of its prayers, of its good works, even of the struggles it has with itself and of the penances it undertakes. So much is this the case that it seeks heavenly delights as ardently as the voluptuary seeks those of this world. By reason of a mercenary and selfish spirit, God is loved solely for the sensible pledges of His love.

And all the time the soul thinks it is loving God for His own sake, with a really disinterested love, whilst deep down it is self and its own satisfaction that is the object of its love. This is proved by the fact that, as soon as God withdraws these sensible joys, the soul becomes unsettled, troubled, despondent and even despairing, and often gives up the struggle, reproaching God for having forsaken it in the first place.

But that is not how God wants to be loved and served. In order to draw and win the soul, He will deign to give it some slight foretastes of its promised happiness, but He will not allow the soul to cling to them or to make them its motive and aim. Most certainly, man is made for happiness, but his real happiness is reserved for the next life. This life is a time of trial, wherein we merit our future happiness. Here below God prepares crosses for His friends, and it is to dispose them to receive them from His hand that He begins by rendering that hand dear to them on account of the favours it bestows. The more delightful and absorbing these favours, the more must we expect the crosses that follow to be heavy and overwhelming.

Let such souls, then, receive gratefully these first favours, and not fear to enjoy them simply. They are milk for babes, food adapted to their frailty. A director who sought to deprive such souls of them, or ordered them to be given up, would be taking away the necessary support and heavenly dew which the soul needs in its present state. But he would be wise to profit by the temporary absences of the heavenly Lover to encourage them to bear such privations calmly. Whilst assuring them that the Bridegroom will return, he must teach them to await patiently His time, and not try to force things to suit their impatience. Let him open their eyes little by little to the meanness of selflove, inspire them with a generous disinterestedness, and lead them to realize that God is infinitely more precious than His gifts; that He must be loved for His own sake, and that in serving Him it is His will alone that the soul seeks. Thus a spirit of detachment will gradually be formed in the soul, so that it will be prepared to accept without fear or danger the time of weaning from sensible sweetness, when God is about to give it more substantial nourishment in the exercise of pure faith.

By pure faith I mean that state in which one serves God without any pledge or assurance of being pleasing to Him. This state is extremely painful to self-love, and so it must be since it is meant to undermine it imperceptibly, and in the end to destroy it so far as is possible in this life. If we were to enter suddenly and without preparation a state so crucifying to nature, we would not be able to bear it, and we would soon be repelled and give up all idea of leading an interior life. And so God, with infinite wisdom, arranges for this transitional stage, and the soul is not weaned until it has achieved a certain growth. And although God may afterwards keep it in an habitual state of privation, yet He tempers its rigours by frequent tokens of His love. The soul, on its part, long remembers the first graces God bestowed upon it, and this remembrance serves as a support in times of desolation. Besides, this state of pure faith has its degrees, and one only arrives at the final stage after many years.

Yet, in spite of this wise economy of grace, few overcome these initial difficulties. Most souls are so soft, sensual and self- centred, that they cannot resolve to give up the consolations of their spiritual childhood. They do their utmost to hold on to them, and when deprived of them for any length of time imagine all is lost. But God takes no notice of their fears. Once He has withdrawn these delights, He restores them only for short periods and at long intervals. He even appears the less disposed to grant them in proportion to the eagerness with which they are sought.

Most persons, therefore, seeing that these privations last longer than they like, lose hope and give up the practice of contemplative prayer, under the plea that the attempt is a waste of time. They relax their vigilance, allow their minds to become distracted, and, despising their Creator, turn back to created things. It is something if they do not fall below what they were when God took them in hand, and merely resume the former practices which they relinquished to follow the leadings of grace. Frequently enough, they become worse than they were before, as a punishment which God allows as a result of their secret despite, pride and despair. They not only give up the interior life, but often enough pious exercises altogether. The senses and passions resume their sway, since they have less strength to resist them. Those who knew them in the time of their first fervour are amazed and scandalized by these falls, which they unjustly attribute to the practice of contemplative prayer, as if it were responsible for the errors consequent upon their having given it up. There are few Christians who run so grave a risk as those who have lapsed from their fervour.

Therefore it is important that those who are called by God to the interior life should know that pure faith is, strictly speaking, the essence of that life, and that the pleasurable state in which they are first placed is only the prelude to and preparation for it. This pure faith glorifies God most, because He is thereby served in a manner worthy of Him, which yields no gratification to self-love, and no opportunity for self-seeking. On the contrary, the soul forgets itself, sacrifices itself, abandons itself to bear whatever rigours it may please a merciful justice to exercise in its regard. If, as St. Paul teaches, the elect are those whom God has predestined to be conformed to the image of His Son; [83] if their holiness increases in proportion to that conformity; if the interior life is that which most resembles the divine pattern: then those who, by God's special favour, are intended for this life must expect that, while on earth, God will treat them as He treated His only Son, having regard to the greatness of His plans and the glory He wishes to receive through them, as well as the glory wherewith He wills to crown them.

Therefore, the sweet peace of the prayer of delight will be followed by long periods of disgust, dryness and weariness, which will render the exercise of prayer as painful as it was formerly pleasant. Perplexity, darkness, anguish and even terror will take the place of light, joy and confidence. We shall feel ourselves the sport of temptations in the matter of purity, faith and hope. We shall continually fancy that we have consented, and nothing will persuade us to the contrary. But we must go on blindly, maybe for a long time, led by obedience, hoping against all hope, loving God without knowing that we love Him or are loved by Him, feeling ourselves rather the object of His displeasure. Not till we have passed through utter darkness shall we find ourselves born again to a new life, which will be the precious pledge of our eternal happiness.

Not all interior souls pass through trials of the same length, or involving equal suffering. God regulates the measure for each as He wills, but all must pass through some form of trial, and indeed are pledged to do so. Their longing for suffering is even greater than their fear; for fear is part of our nature, whereas desire is in the will. The love of the cross is one of the first things God implants in the soul, and that love goes on ever increasing.

You, then, who are entering on the state of pure faith, gird yourself to endure bravely the first absences of your Beloved, and thus merit His support when He visits you with His crosses. Rest assured that if you are faithful, He will lead you as far as you are able to go and He will lay more crosses on you than you will ask for. He tries severely those who love Him, in order that they may love Him more. At the same time, He communicates to them an unseen strength. And it is certain, though it sounds incredible, that the more they suffer, the more these souls enjoy a peace which, as St. Paul says, surpasses all understanding. [84] Besides supporting them, God inspires them with words which have the power to support others weaker than themselves. St. Paul bore witness to this in his own case, when he said: Who comforteth us in all our tribulation, that we may be able to comfort them who are in distress. [85]

But do not let what I have said frighten you: it is but a picture of the purgatory of love. What would it be like if I traced for you a picture of the purgatory of justice, which all must pass through after death, if they have not been purified before? One must be purified in one or the other, and we cannot thank God enough if we are able in this life to arrive at that degree of purity which the soul must acquire before it can see God.

You dread trials. But they are absolutely unavoidable if you are to enter heaven; and the willing acceptance of them will make them sweet. You do not appreciate the all-powerful work of grace, and the wondrous changes it brings to pass in the mind and heart. Yield yourself up to it, have no fear for your own weakness: you will be weak only in so far as you rely on yourself. If you place your whole trust in God alone, you will be able to say with St. Paul: I can do all things in Him Who strengtheneth me. [86]

You will ask me: why must we suffer so many interior and exterior trials? Can we not be saints at a lesser price? The answer is No. The Gospel affirms that sanctity is only to be attained through suffering; or at least, by the will to suffer. It consists in the readiness to embrace all the crosses that it may please God to send us. God does not require that we should forestall crosses, but it is His will that we should expect them with a firm heart, and accept them bravely when they come.

At such a cost, then, you will say, I would rather not be a saint, provided I can be saved. Foolish soul! You dwell on the fleeting evils of this life, and are blind to the exceeding weight of glory and happiness awaiting you. [87] Niggardly in what concerns your best interests, you would barter heaven for what costs you little, afraid to bid too highly for it. Base and sordid soul! You only consider yourself, and will do nothing for God. Do you realize what your salvation cost Our Lord? And yet you complain of what it will cost you! You are content to be saved, but will you, if you refuse to be a saint? Are you sure that you will do enough, and only just enough, to ensure your salvation? Ought you not rather to fear doing too little than too much?

Besides, supposing you do manage to be saved, does that mean that you will escape suffering? Is there no Purgatory; and who is it meant for if not for you? Can you enter heaven without the purification of that fire, which must consume all that remains of your self-love? I cannot insist too much on this point, which to the eye of faith is conclusive.

To return to the subject of dryness, I would only add this. Those who suffer from it are very subject to distractions. But these are inevitable, and torture many good souls who fancy them wilful, and cannot get rid of them, no matter what they do.

For the comfort of such persons, I would beg them to remember that no distraction is sinful unless it arises in the will, and is fostered in the heart. It is not a real distraction if, contrary to our will, the mind wanders on to another subject than that on which it intended to dwell. I go to my prayer fully intending to adore God and to unite myself to Him. Without any warning, my imagination goes off at a tangent, and is occupied with a thousand different things. If I do not want these distractions, and they distress me; if, as soon as I am aware of them, I recall my thoughts gently to the subject of my meditation or, better still, remain quietly in the presence of God, then they are not voluntary, because my intention to adore God and be united to Him has never changed. Even if the whole time of my prayer passes in this way, my prayer is none the less pleasing in God's sight.

We are not responsible for the thoughts that enter our minds, but it does depend upon our will whether we entertain them or not, and also on the general disposition of our mind at other times. If we allow too much freedom to the senses and imagination, or let the mind get excited by all sorts of subjects, and dissipate our energies by the exercise of foolish curiosity, or by frivolous conversations and idle thoughts; if we are not careful to keep our heart free from all desires and undue attachments, we must not be surprised if in time of prayer we find it difficult to be recollected, and that all these thoughts come back to us. For such distractions we are responsible, even if at the moment we yield no consent to them, because we have caused them knowingly.

But if, in the course of the day, we keep a curb on our senses and imagination, if we attend carefully to the duties of our state, if we suffer nothing to divert us from the sense of God's presence, which is what should occupy our hearts, then we may disregard all distractions that intrude on our time of prayer, provided we do not consent to them. Moreover, it may be assumed that we do not consent to them, if we live in a state of habitual recollection. These rules are simple and adapted to cure any scruples with regard to attention at prayer, whether vocal or mental.

Usually we bring to our prayer the same state of mind in which we are accustomed to live. God will not work a miracle to keep us recollected, and we will in vain endeavour to be so if at other times we suffer our mind and heart to wander as they please.

I must add a word for those who have been raised by God to passive prayer, and are in a state of dryness. First, it is impossible in this state to be absolutely free from the wanderings of the imagination. If God inspires no holy thought in the mind and kindles no warmth in the heart, we are bound to feel, as it were, lost, with the result that the imagination has a free field. But if we watch, we will notice that these thoughts are vague and inconsequent, and do not affect the will, and leave no trace behind them. Afterwards, we find it difficult to recall them, which is a sure sign that they were involuntary.

In the second place, these distractions, far from being harmful, can be profitable to the soul, since they try it and encourage it, both to feel its own misery and to bear with it patiently. It is very painful for a devout soul to feel that it has become the sport of the imagination, to lose its recollectedness, and to be given over to all sorts of vain thoughts during prayer. But these things keep us humble, by showing us what we are, and making us realize that of our own endeavours we cannot obtain one good thought or feeling. Involuntary and habitual distractions are a proof of this, and prevent us from taking any credit to ourselves, when we experience a little relief.

Self-love creeps in everywhere. If we feel any sensible emotions during prayer and communion, we are apt to grow self-complacent; to take pleasure in them, and so spoil the purity of our intention. In a state of dryness, self-love has no support, and is therefore wounded and perturbed. But we must take no notice of its complaints and grumblings, and the false reasonings whereby it endeavours to perplex us. Let it cry out against an interior state where all is for God, and nothing for itself. The proof that this aridity is profitable to our spiritual advancement is that, under its action, nature suffers and is gradually exhausted and destroyed, while the life of grace increases and gains strength.

In the third place, these distractions form part of God's plan. He makes use of them to hide His action in the soul, which is thus deterred from looking at itself, and seeing what is going on. When it enjoys any sensible peace, and all its powers are held in a deep calm, it is sure to dwell upon its state with feelings of too strong attachment and pleasure. This is not what God wants. And that is why He gradually removes all that induces this condition, and allows the soul to become apparently a prey to distractions, while He works within it secretly, without the soul being aware of its progress.

Beware, then, of losing patience or hope when the imagination thus runs wild. Do not suppose that your prayer is worse or less pleasing to God. Do not listen to yourself or to the devil, who would like to induce you to give it up as a waste of time. Do not take up a book for the purpose of occupying your mind. Directors should never recommend such a practice to souls in this state. That would be to want to lead them back to meditation from which God has already called them. Neither should you strain yourself or weary your mind or body in order to drive away these distractions. Such efforts are useless. Far from calming the imagination, they only irritate and excite it all the more, just as flies perpetually driven away only return all the more persistently. Despise these things, let them drop of themselves, and do not let them disturb your peace. Be content with mentioning them to your confessor, but not as sins. Above all, do not worry yourself as to whether you have given your consent to them or not.

If you keep your mind thus at rest in the midst of your ordinary distractions, you will be given the grace to remain at peace when you are assailed by sterner temptations, which God may permit, for your greater good, in the time of prayer, which is the time the devil usually chooses for his worst attacks. If you act as I have advised (for the rules are more or less the same for temptations as for distractions), you will have nothing to fear. The devil will be put to rout, and all his attempts to make you give up will only cause you to hold on all the more firmly, and advance more surely.

But this question of temptations calls for a maxim and explanation of its own.

82.   Cf. Ps. xxxiii. 9
83.   Rom. viii. 29
84.   Phil. iv.
85.   Cf. 2 Cor. I. 4
86.   Phil. iv. 13
87.   Cf. 2 Cor. iv. 17

Sixteenth Maxim: Temptations

The tempter combines cunning with violence: we must meet him with prayer and vigilance.

The devil has little hold on souls that are given to prayer and mortification. The most common temptations hardly affect them, since they forbid them entrance. Should they be occasionally taken by surprise, it is because they are momentarily off their guard; and as a rule there are no grave consequences. And it is not the devil who is the principal instrument in such cases, for every man, says St. James, is tempted by his own concupiscence, being drawn away and allured. [88] Such souls are thus only usually exposed to these temptations in so far as God permits them in order to purify their conscience, exercise their patience, deepen their humility, increase their merit, and add brightness to their crown. It is of such temptations that I now propose to speak.

In the first place, I think we are unnecessarily afraid of them. It would be presumptuous to defy the devil, but it is a sign of weakness to be afraid of him. As St. Augustine says, he is a chained dog, who can bark and worry, but he cannot bite if we keep out of his reach. Such lively apprehension may arise from different causes. The imagination has a lot to do with it. We are struck by what we have read in the lives of certain saints, and fancy we are going to pass through the same experiences, and be driven, as they were, to the last extremity. Take courage, timid soul! Great temptations are only for brave hearts; do not be so vain as to suppose that God is going to treat you as He treated such chosen souls, who are very few in number.

This fear may also arise from a craven spirit. Such hearts are narrow, wanting in generosity, and incapable of great sacrifices. They tremble at the least danger; all they ask for is a sweet and untroubled piety, sheltered from the storms and blasts. No sooner do the winds blow, the skies darken, and the thunders roll, than they imagine the whole of their spiritual edifice is about to totter. Faint-hearted soldiers, indeed! You would like to conquer, but you do not want to fight. The mere sight of the enemy puts you to flight. Complete victory is reserved only for those who resist unto blood.

This fear also arises from a want of trust in God. If we trusted absolutely to His strength, we would have nothing to fear; for what have we to be afraid of, if God the all-powerful is on our side? The Lord is my light and my salvation, says the Psalmist, whom shall I fear? The Lord is the protector of my life, of whom shall I be afraid? ... If armies in camp should stand together against me, my heart shall not fear. If a battle should rise up against me, in this will I be confident. [89]

But instead of keeping our eyes on Our Lord, we look only at ourselves. We measure our strength against that of our tempter and, being only too conscious of our weakness, we lay down our arms and turn our back before the battle has even begun. We pretend that this is humility and a prudent distrust of self, but it is not. It is self-love and presumption, which attributes success to our courage, instead of expecting it from God alone. In our blindness, we do not reflect that God's time for helping us is when the testing comes. Before that, it would be useless and dangerous to deem ourselves strong, as St. Peter did. But when the moment arrives, God will help us, and will do so the more, the more we put our trust in Him.

And why should we fear temptations? Do we not know that they are necessary for us, since without them we can make no progress in the way of perfection? Of course they are necessary to strengthen us in the very virtues which they assail. We will never reach a high degree of purity, faith, hope, or love for God or our neighbour, unless we are strongly exercised in these virtues. Our Lord taught that it is the storm that proves the stability of a house; [90] that if the house be built on a rock, far from being overthrown, it will be all the stronger. The temptations by which the devil seeks to rob us of our virtues, render those virtues all the dearer to us. We make greater efforts to retain them, and quicken and multiply our prayers that God may be pleased to preserve us from their loss.

Temptations, moreover, are necessary in order that we may know ourselves as we really are. What doth he know that hath not been tried, says the son of Sirach. [91] We must have faced the enemy, and that more than once; have experienced the force of his stratagems and of his onslaughts; have been tempted again and again to give in, before we can appreciate that we can do nothing without God, and all things with Him. [92] Before the battle, we are either cowardly or presumptuous; it is only in the thick of it that we learn really to know ourselves. Should we be overcome, defeat brings with it humility. If, despite all resistance and foresight, we feel ourselves on the point of giving in, we realize better the greater need to call upon God for help. If, just when we think we are irrevocably lost, God suddenly delivers us from our peril, the very risk we have run forces us to realize that it is to Him we owe the victory.

Temptations are necessary in order that we may learn not to trust in our own strength. When the violence of the temptation is extreme; when our strength is exhausted through long resistance; when we see no way of escape and nothing seems left to us but to surrender: then, seeing no hope in ourselves and having no further defence, we must needs throw ourselves into the arms of God. This is just the moment God has been waiting for, and never more than now shall we receive His help. He has forced the issue, precisely to show us that He alone can save us from destruction, even though it seems inevitable. He loves to bring us back from the very gates of death. The Lord killeth and maketh alive, it is written, He bringeth down to hell, and bringeth back again. [93]

Finally, temptations are necessary to bring us into closer union with God. When do we call upon Him with greater fervour than when 'our feet are almost gone, and our steps have well-nigh slipped'? When do we hide in His bosom, if not when the enemy threatens to deprive us of the life of grace? When all seems well, we forget to think about God. It is only when temptation recalls us to Him that we cling to Him, and will not let Him go.

As for those whom God has destined for the guidance of others, temptations are essential for them, since there is no better teacher than experience. They are able to feel more compassion for those who are tempted, and are more patient with them. They understand the tactics of the devil, they dread neither his deceits nor his open attacks. They know with what weapons to oppose him, and how to prevent and frustrate his plans. They are in a position to encourage others, and to give them salutary advice. A director who has not passed through similar trials has not the same advantage. He is timid, hesitating, uncertain how to decide. He bewilders those who apply to him or, what is worse, he misunderstands their state, judges them culpable and treats them harshly; he repels them, and drives them almost to despair.

You fear temptations? But God is faithful, Who will not suffer you to be tempted above that which you are able; but will make also with temptation issue, that you may be able to bear it. [94] Let us ponder a moment on these words of St. Paul.

God is faithful. That is to say, He always does what He promises. He wills that the love of His children should be put to the test, and so allows the devil to tempt them. At the same time, He has promised to come to our aid. And what can all the efforts of hell avail if God is with us? [95] If we turn to Him with confidence in our hour of need, and do not abandon Him He will never abandon us. The devil wants to harm us and turn us away from God; God's intention is to strengthen us, and make us advance in virtue, by the very things in which we are tempted. The devil can do nothing of himself, and can only tempt us with God's permission and within its limits. Moreover, as St. Paul reminds us, God will not allow us to be tempted beyond our strength. His justice, His faithfulness, His loving kindness are all opposed to such a thing. Therefore, before allowing us to be tempted, He waits until we have attained a certain degree of strength. He does not bring us face to face with the enemy right at the beginning of our course, while our efforts are still weak and hesitating, and the least rebuff might be too much for us. He prepares us from afar for the combat; He forms and inures us before confronting us with the enemy.

Besides this, He gives us the help we need at the time: He is at our side. Not only does He inspire us with courage, but He fights with us. The grace He gives us then is always sufficient to assure us the victory, and even make us always superior to the enemy, unless, by our presumption or want of trust, by our negligence or infidelity, we are ourselves the cause that it becomes a sufficient help and no more, with which God foresees that we shall fall.

For God is always faithful. And even when we refuse the special grace of which we have shown ourselves unworthy and with which we would have been victorious, He gives us an ordinary grace, but one strong enough to save us from a fall, although in fact it does not do so through our own fault.

When, therefore, we are faithful on our part; when we have not done anything to deprive ourselves of His special help, God will always see to it that the temptation serves for our advance, the struggle being followed by victory. This is what God wants, and He will, on His side, do all that is necessary to assure our victory, provided we place no obstacle in His way.

Let me add that the goodness of God is so great, as well as His power, that He wills to, and can, make our very reverses turn to our spiritual advantage, if we turn to Him with a sincere and loving repentance, to which He invites us with the strongest advances and the most pressing motives. Thus even the falls of David and St. Peter, being turned to good account, contributed to their sanctification.

Why then, need you fear temptations, if your trust in God is all that it should be? You complain that these temptations beset you during your time of prayer and at Holy Communion; that the devil chooses precisely these times to attack you. Say rather, that God permits you to be tempted just when you are best prepared to resist evil; when your immediate intention is to unite yourself to Him; when Jesus present in your heart will Himself repel the assaults of the devil.

But, you say, this deprives me of peace in prayer. Very probably your soul may then be agitated and troubled on the surface, but it depends on yourself whether its depths are calm. It is not in the devil's power to touch the depths of the soul, which is the true seat of peace. You may lose the sense of calm, but that does you no harm. It is for you to hold on to the reality.

But, again you will say, it keeps me from going to communion. Why should it? You have only a more pressing reason for going. The devil insinuates the feeling which would keep you away, only because he knows what strength you obtain from it, and how certain is his defeat if you meet him in that strength. Indeed, the most violent temptations subside and fade away the moment we receive the adorable Body of Christ. I do not know that it ever happened that immediately after receiving Holy Communion anyone, no matter how tormented by the most frightful thoughts beforehand, did not find himself relieved from them

Again you say: the devil suggests images, thoughts; desires, that fill my mind with horror. So much the better, if his suggestions do fill your mind with horror, for then it is a manifest proof that you reject them, and that God rejects them in you. Do you not recall that Our Lord said: From the heart come forth evil thoughts? [96] That means that our thoughts are only evil when the heart conceives, encourages and takes pleasure in them. How, then, can your thoughts be evil when your heart abhors them? Sin lies, not in having an object present to the mind or

impressed upon it, but in the consent given by the will; and
nothing is more opposed to this consent than such a state of
mind as yours.

'But I seem to have no strength whatever to resist such
temptations'. Since they fill you with horror, and you would
rather die than take the least pleasure in them, you do
resist, and that with all the strength of your will. You may
not realize it, but your will is in spite of everything, most
active. Judge for yourself by the result. God has reasons for
not letting you know that you are resisting, as you are in
fact doing, because He does not want you to attribute the
victory to your own efforts, and grow vain and self-
complacent on the strength of it. He does not want you to
say: 'I was tempted, and I resisted' but 'it was not I who
fought, but God, Who fought and gained the victory for
me'. Are you not glad that the honour should be given
where it is due, and that God has placed you in the happy
position of being unable to deny it?

'Yet it seems to me that I have given my consent'. On what
grounds? 'Because the temptation lasted so long'. That is
not a reason. It merely proves that it was a long testing time
for you. Or is it because you thought you took pleasure in
it? There is such a thing as involuntary pleasure, an
impression on the senses, which is the natural effect of
certain temptations. A heated imagination may be the
cause, or it may be the devil. But the pleasure felt and the
impression made are not the same thing as consent.
However, decide nothing on your own. You are in no state
to make any decision while you are disturbed. And once the
temptation has passed, do not think about it any more. It is
very dangerous to go over the whole thing again, and
masters ofthe spiritual life are unanimous in forbidding it.
Refer the matter to your confessor, and once he has given a

general decision, and if necessary repeated it, be perfectly at peace.

The Christian's arms against the devil are watchfulness and prayer. Watch ye, and pray that ye enter not into temptation. [97] Our Lord does not say: in order that you may be kept from temptation, but in order that it may not enter your heart, and that you may not succumb to it. Vigilance is necessary against an enemy who is as clever as he is violent; who, as a roaring lion goeth about seeking whom he may devour. [98] Vigilance is necessary for everyone, no matter how holy. Anyone not on his guard, therefore, is for that very reason in danger from temptation, and the danger is greater for a good man who presumes on his strength than for a sinner who dreads the consequences of his weakness. Remember Our Lord's words when He recommended vigilance to the apostles: What I say to you, I say to all: Watch! [99] Vigilance is necessary always. The enemy is ever lying in ambush, and never sleeps. He awaits the moment to take us off our guard, and he is as quick to do so as he is clever to know the moment.

This vigilance consists in the first place in avoiding occasions of temptation. One must never wilfully expose oneself to temptation, under any pretext whatsoever. In ancient times, the bishops were not at all anxious for Christians to expose themselves to martyrdom, nor even to declare themselves without necessity.

Several were known to have renounced their faith when under torment, having thus declared themselves through an indiscreet zeal. If, therefore, holy prudence did not allow them to seek martyrdom, even more so were even the most holy among them forbidden to venture on any deed fraught with peril, without being assured that it was God's will.

And even when it was clearly God's will, they had to place all their trust in Him, so that the fear of danger might not weaken their resolution.

In the second place, vigilance consists in a humble distrust of oneself. The Lord is the keeper of the little ones, says David: I was humbled and He delivered me. [100] He who is lowly in his own eyes, and relies on God alone, will as surely not fail, as he who trusts in his own strength is bound to be discomfited. To the latter, even victory would be harmful, because of the presumption to which it would give rise, and it might even lead eventually to an irretrievable fall. No man shall prevail by his own strength, we read in the Book of Kings. [101] If God, then, is our strength, equally must our trust be in Him.

But do not confound, as many do, mistrust of self with faint- heartedness. A faint-hearted man looks only at himself and, comparing his danger with his weakness, turns his back on it, when what he should do is to face it. The true Christian distrust of self, while being aware of its own frailty, looks to God for its strength, and when God calls it to battle fears naught. Indeed, on the contrary, the more it feels its own incapacity for resisting, the more certain is it that the divine strength will sustain it. When I am weak, says the apostle, then am I powerful. [102] And again: I can do all things in Him Who strengtheneth me. [103]

Vigilance consists, moreover, in a constant fidelity. Never give up the practice of interior prayer and mortification. Follow exactly the guidance God has given you in this matter, even in the smallest things. Observe in every particular the rule laid down for you, or that you have embraced. Allow yourself no wilful breach of it, and the devil will have no power over you. His very assaults will turn to his own confusion.

Above all, try always to remain calm in time of temptation. Do not let your mind dwell on what is passing within you, and never argue with the devil. You will only be entangled with your own thoughts if you do, and you will be caught in his snares. Keep close to God and let the storm pass. Your anxiety and arguing will only increase the tempest and make it last longer. And when it has passed, quietly continue on your way, without scrutinizing yourself to see if you have taken any pleasure in it, or given your consent.

To vigilance Our Lord would have you join prayer; and both must be continuous. We ought always to pray and not to faint, says St. Luke. [104] This continual prayer is, as has been said elsewhere, but the directing of the heart towards God, and the heart's secret cry for help. The devil cannot harm a soul thus disposed, and ever shielded by the buckler of prayer.

Besides the general attitude of prayer, however, which should be the soul's habitual state, it is a good practice, in times of temptation, to take refuge if possible in your oratory, or in the presence of the Blessed Sacrament. If that is not possible, then at least have recourse to ejaculatory prayers, which are as so many arrows wherewith to wound the foe. And let these prayers be calm and submissive, and full of trust. Do not ask impatiently for the temptation to pass, for such a request may come from self- love. You are humiliated at being subjected to such horrible thoughts, and you would like to shake off the feeling. But humiliation is one of the best effects of temptations, and that is why God permits them. Yield yourself up wholly, therefore, to God, and bear with the temptations as long as God wants you to.

He alone knows what good is wrought by them. He has a fixed time for relieving you of them, and that will take place as soon as you have profited by them as fully as it is His will that you should. Three times St. Paul asked to be delivered from an annoying temptation, which God permitted in order that he might not fall into the sin of vainglory, because of the greatness of the revelations given him. And what was Our Lord's answer? My grace is sufficient for thee; for power is thus made perfect in infirmity. [105]

For temptations are the counterpoise of graces received, and our graces are always in exact proportion to our temptations. We delight in graces that raise us up, and we fear temptations that humiliate us. But such humiliation is itself a grace, indeed a greater grace than that which we previously enjoyed, for it shields us against those dangers to which we might otherwise be exposed. That is why God allows us to be tempted, and His infinite power is all the more apparent by reason of our weakness.

Now however horrible and humiliating our temptations, we must never hide them from our spiritual guide. We must open our heart to him, and keep nothing back. God will bless such frankness, which is in itself a great act of humility to which many graces are attached. It will also inspire the director to strengthen and encourage us as he sees fit. The devil will do all he can to silence those he tempts, confident that he will succeed if only he can persuade them to say nothing about the matter.

Be faithful, then, and from your guide you will receive peace and light and strength. His decisions will calm you, his counsels bring you light, and his exhortations give you fresh courage. Having explained your case to him in all simplicity, abide by his advice with complete confidence. Do not allow yourself to judge otherwise than he has decided, not even in thought. Do not say: I did not make my case clear; or, he did not understand me. There is no end to that kind of argument. Acquiesce and submit. Moreover, be strictly faithful in observing all he tells you, whether it be to help you to avoid temptations, or to weaken or overcome them altogether.

88. James I. 14
89. Ps. xxvi. 1-3
90. Cf. Matt. vii. 24-25
91. Ecclus. xxxiv. 9
92. Cf. John xv. 5 and Phil. iv. 13
93. I Kings ii. 6.
94. I Cor. x. 13
95. Cf. Rom. viii. 31
96. Matt. xv. 19
97. Matt. xxvi. 41
98. I Peter v. 8
99. Mark xiii. 37
100. Ps. cxiv. 6
101. I Kings ii. 9
102. 2 Cor. xii. 10
103. Phil. iv. 13
104. Luke xviii. 1
105. 2 Cor. xii. 9

Seventeenth Maxim: Self-love

Beware of self-love, the rival of the love of God.

Nothing indicates better the nature of self-love, or should make it more hateful to us, than the idea that it is the rival of the love of God. Homines sunt voluntates, says St. Augustine: men are their wills. We can bestow our whole love on but one only of two objects: God or self. If we put God first and refer all things to Him, then His love will make us good and pleasing in His sight, imparting a supernatural value to all our actions, and perfecting us as we grow in purity and simplicity. If, on the other hand, we refer everything to ourselves, our self-love will upset God's order in us, rendering us most displeasing to Him, vitiating actions otherwise holy, and lowering us in proportion to the sway it exercises in our hearts.

These two loves are entirely opposed to one another. They are not only rivals but enemies, disputing the possession of our heart. No compact or truce is possible between them; they hate one another, attack and persecute each other to the death. The total extinction of self-love, either in this world or in the next, opens heaven to us and ensures our eternal happiness; whilst the extinction of the love of God in our heart, when we pass out of this life, is hell and constitutes our eternal misery.

When a Christian really gives himself to God and to His service, divine love takes possession of his heart, sets up its throne therein and at once proceeds to drive out self-love, the latter resisting with all its strength Attacked and driven from one place to another, it takes refuge wherever it can, retreating from hold to hold until it hides in the innermost recesses of the soul. This is its last refuge, from which it is extremely difficult to dislodge it. There is no device by which it does not endeavour to harm and weaken its assailant, and to lessen, if it cannot prevent, its ultimate victory. It is always dangerous, even after defeat; and often, when we think we have crushed it, it will arise more formidable than ever.

Such is the enemy we have to fight, with the help of grace: an enemy born with us, and in some way part of our very self. Age, passions, habits, thoughts--all, even our good qualities and occasionally our virtues, contribute to strengthen its hold upon us, and drive it deeper. It is so involved with ourselves that it seems almost impossible to distinguish it, and to attempt to destroy it is to jeopardize our very existence.

How powerless we are in the presence of an enemy so much a part of ourselves, and that has such power over us. What is worse is that it blinds us, and deprives us of the very means of recognizing it. It is only in the light of grace that we can discern it, and become aware of its wiles. That light alone enables us to foresee its blows, teaches us how to ward them off, and strengthens us to do battle with it. If we pay no heed to this light, or lose it through our own fault, we are left wholly defenceless, unable not only to conquer but even to resist; unable to see our enemy or to regard him as such. Indeed, we are so deceived as to look upon him as our greatest friend.

This wretched blindness is common to all men, even to the devout. It is the more baneful since it is unperceived and unsuspected. This is so much the case, that we have the greatest difficulty in convincing ourselves of its existence and presence. We are all more or less in the condition of the Pharisees who, with regard to Our Lord, were blinded by arrogant self-love, and yet fancied themselves clear-sighted. Our Lord told them: You say that you see, and therefore your sin remaineth. [106] By their wilfulness they filled up the measure of the iniquity which they should have abhored.

We may assume as a fact, without fear of contradiction, that we are blind on many points concerning our perfection, and perhaps our salvation. We should pray continuously for God to enlighten us, either directly by His Holy Spirit, or indirectly by the advice of our friends or by the reproaches of our enemies. In whatever way light may come, it is always a blessing sent by God, and we should welcome and receive it gratefully, encouraging others to offer it, and neglecting nothing that may lead us to profit by it. This is a disposition that we can never pray for enough, and one to which most of our natural tendencies are opposed. We must be on our guard, I will not say against flattery (I presume our director or spiritual friends would hardly be guilty of such a thing), but even against marks of consideration and respect, especially if our rank, age or temperament would seem to warrant them. We should take it for granted that our faults are glossed over or made light of, out of discretion or kindness; that if we are praised, it is not for the good we do, but in order to encourage us to do better. If we are blamed, we may well add to the faults others find in us; and if we are praised, we should at least discredit much of the praise. It is only in this way that we shall keep a check on ourselves, and on the deadly enemy within us.

But now let us examine a little more closely the various devices that self-love employs in order to corrupt or lessen true devotion. Its subtlest aim is to appropriate to itself the work of grace; to rob God of the glory of our good actions, or at least to claim some share in them, and deprive us of the merit which derives from humility. 'Beware of me as of a big thief' St. Philip Neri used to say to Our Lord. Self-love is jealous of God's claims, and will do anything to rob Him of them. These claims are concerned for the glory that belongs to Him alone, and which He can concede to no one. He allows us the use of His gifts, but the glory must revert to Him in its entirety. And it is just this glory that self-love covets. Self-love wants us to glory in ourselves, against the express command of the apostle: He that glorieth, let him glory in the Lord. [107]

But thinking to enrich us at the expense of God, in actual fact self-love does the very opposite. For there is no merit, no reward, no blessing, save for those who, recognizing their spiritual poverty, attribute nothing and appropriate nothing to themselves, but give thanks to God for all the good that is in them, referring it all to Him Who gave it. God is jealous, and the chief effect of His jealousy is that, as every good gift proceeds from Him, so it is His will that man should render Him homage for it, and acknowledge that he holds all from the hand of God. And, indeed, it is only right that a pauper who owes everything to God should never forget that he is poor by nature, and possesses nothing that has not come to him through the liberality of his benefactor. If he becomes proud, and asserts that he has a right to everything, then he deserves to lose all.

Self-love is mercenary. In the service of God, it looks to its own interests without rising to higher considerations. A soul tainted with this poison, desires holiness as an embellishing ornament and a distinguishing perfection. It desires to be pure, but only in order to contemplate its own purity. It fears sin, less as an offence against God than as a disfigurement of the brilliancy of its own beauty. It is more astonished than abashed by its faults, scarcely conceiving

how it was possible for it to fall. Its repentance savours
more of vexation than of regret, and what it believes to be
an act of contrition and love of God is merely an act of
inordinate self-love.

Self-love is greedy for consolations. It seeks them from
God and from men. It enjoys them with clinging eagerness,
regrets them bitterly when deprived of them, and if the
privation lasts too long for its fancy relaxes its fidelity,
complains and murmurs and threatens to give up altogether,
as if God merited to be served only for His gifts. And all
the time, it is clever enough to persuade us that we are
generous, disinterested and actuated by the purest love of
God.

Self-love is vain and presumptuous in times of spiritual
abundance and prosperity. At such times, it presumes on its
strength and thinks itself capable of anything. It makes
much of its promises and protestations to God, in spite of
the fact that they all end in empty words, which it produces
as solid proofs of its devotion! But let want and adversity
come, and immediately it is cast down and in despair, and
incapable of the slightest effort. Before the combat, it is
valiant enough; it defies its enemies and overcomes them,
but all in its own fancy. When actually engaged in battle, it
is timid and trembles, and flees at the first appearance of
danger.

It loves the sort of holiness that is quiet and comfortable,
easy- going and involving suffering to neither mind nor
body, and where there are few obstacles to overcome: the
kind of holiness that can be acquired quickly and at little
cost or for the mere wishing. (St. Francis of Sales used to
liken it to a cloak which one slips on lightly). But this is all
only a dream. Selflove would like to be holy, but will do

nothing to become so. It is soft, indolent, lazy, full of indeterminate desires, impatient, put off by the least difficulty, weary and exhausted at the slightest effort. Do not talk to it about climbing steep ascents: the path it likes is an easy gradient. So long as there is no real effort to be made, all is well; but if the struggle calls for the least contradiction to a favourite tendency, the overcoming of a repugnance, the resisting of a temptation, it loses courage, stops short and turns back.

Self-love will have nothing to do with virtue which is humble, hidden and unnoticed by others; still less, when it is despised, calumniated and persecuted. Good deeds done in secret and with no sounding of trumpets are not to its liking. It loves to appear in full daylight. It seeks display, recognition, esteem and applause, which it obtains craftily, invites deprecatingly, receives hypocritically, and enjoys immensely, all the time pretending to reject these things, knowing very well that if the world refuses them, it will make up for it itself in secret.

It hates simplicity and ordinary everyday life. It affects singularity, and defines sanctity not as the faithful performance of one's normal duties but as something out of the ordinary. There is nothing regular, sustained or constant in its habits; all is fanciful, capricious and inconsequent. It is always wanting to make sure that it has done well, that its conduct is approved by God, and still more by the director. Hence arise ever repeated introspections, restless and scrupulous testings of motives and intentions, an unceasing exaction of approbation, from one's own conscience, from God in prayer, and from the director in the confessional and elsewhere. All this, so it asserts, in order to gain firmness, support and encouragement: a vain pretext! It is all done with the purpose of finding occasion for self- gratulation, food for vanity, or at least an assurance of progress made, and the comfort of some light on the weary darkness of a way which provides no visible support.

Self-love is ever occupied with making comparisons. It exults in superiority, is vexed and annoyed if forced to yield to others. It censures everybody's conduct except its own. Its own way of prayer must be the best. Or else it envies souls which it supposes to be more advanced and more favoured by God. It notes the faults in others, criticizes their actions, judges and condemns motives, and is always whispering to itself 'I would not have acted thus; I would not have spoken thus in the same circumstances!' Its most terrible characteristic is the spiritual jealousy which gnaws and tortures it. Persons thus affected think that their director never pays them sufficient attention. They regard themselves as neglected, while every notice is lavished on others. They watch to see how often the director speaks to them, how often he writes to them, visits them, how long he stays with them. There is no end to their complaints on this score, and if they receive, or think they receive, no satisfaction, their irritation knows no bounds. They even extend the effects of their miserable jealousy to God Himself, sometimes accusing Him of treating others better than He treats them. They proclaim their innocence, how commendable their conduct is and their austerities, and, like the prodigal son's elder brother in the Gospel, reproach the Father for having shown favour to those who have not served Him half so faithfully as they have done.

Self-love accustoms the soul to claim as its own those gifts and graces with which God endows it, telling the soul that it has a right to them. And so when God appears to withdraw them, it becomes most impatient and does all it can to hold on to them. But God does not really despoil the soul of these gifts; He always leaves in the soul the roots of virtue (but in such wise that the soul is no longer aware of them), in order that it may cease to look upon them as its own. To this end He allows temptations contrary to these virtues, feelings of distaste and strong repugnance in exercising them, upheavals of passion in one's lower nature. To these the soul does not really consent, although it may think it does. For God withdraws all power of self-appreciation, even the recognition of such acts as are really virtuous.

Lastly, self-love robs God of His right to be the soul's centre, a right which it would take to itself. This appropriation is a deep- seated and radical vice, which has become so much a part of man's nature that he has great difficulty in recognizing it, in appreciating its mischievous character, and in consenting that God should deliver him from it. However advanced a soul may be, it could never give up this secret reference to self, which leads it to consider both its perfection and its happiness from a selfish point of view and not subordinate (as it should be) to the will and glory of God: it would never make this renunciation, I say, if God, in order to force its consent, did not exercise that absolute control which the soul has given Him over its free-will. That is self-love's last stronghold, and its deepest hiding place. It is of this that St. Francis of Sales said that we are fortunate if this vice dies a quarter of an hour before we do.

Self-love is the one source of all the illusions of the spiritual life. By its means the devil exercises his deceits, leads souls astray, drags them sometimes to hell by the very road that seems to lead them to heaven. We long eagerly for spiritual delights; the devil provides false ones, which encourage vanity and sensuality. We desire ardently extraordinary favours; the devil transforms himself into a angel of light, and counterfeits the divine operations. We question God, curious to find out our own state and that of others, and about secret and future events; the devil causes us to hear an inward voice, which we take for an answer from heaven. We fancy ourselves recipients of special lights, and grow wilful, obstinate and deaf to good advice. We throw off the yoke of authority, and under the deceitful guise of sanctity conceal the pride of Lucifer.

I have only stated the abuses and disorders introduced by self- love into devotion. I shall not enter into the specious reasonings with which self-love skilfully conceals itself. It is much too wary to appear in its true colours, for then it would be manifestly too despicable and odious, and one would be ashamed to pay any attention to it. It assumes the fairest of hues, and the most seductive disguises. Its motive is always zeal for God's glory, its aim the perfection of one's own soul, or the spiritual welfare of others. Its real purpose lies hidden in the depths of the heart. It professes other objects which are good and holy, and by adroitly intermingling them is able to pass them off on us.

The remedy for so great an evil is to become, in our devotion, attached to nothing that appeals to the senses, but to rise above all things and cleave to God alone and His good pleasure. We are always safe, provided we look at things from God's point of view, not ours. That is why the way of pure faith wherein we walk, as it were, blindly and without anything to reassure us, shields us from all illusions. That also is why God hides His work from us so carefully, and forbids us to pry into it. Self-love would like to have a finger in it all, to see everything, so that it can find something to feed on. So God, for the very opposite reason, hides all He is doing from it.

Cease, then, from all disquieting reflections on yourself, and never examine yourself from motives of curiosity, complacency or self-interest. Forget yourself and rest wholly in God, and endeavour to put into practice what Our Lord said one day to St. Catherine of Siena: My daughter, think of Me, and I will think of you: a short phrase but a profound one, in which is comprised all perfection. In other words, God will concern Himself with our true interests, if we will occupy ourselves with His. Oh how pure and happy that soul would be if, taking no thought for itself and lost in God, it had no other object than His glory and the accomplishment of His will. All the faults that we commit in the interior life, all that retards our progress, the obstacles we meet, all the anxiety, the torments that try us, derive from the fact that we look at ourselves instead of looking at God, and trusting in all things in His goodness, His wisdom and His love.

I am aware that perfect forgetfulness of self is only to be attained by slow degrees. But it must be our continual aim and we must exercise ourselves in acts of that virtue at every opportunity. Such opportunities are not rare, since we have ourselves with us always. 'Wherever you find yourself, there leave yourself' says the Imitation. The practical application of this precept is almost limitless. It is very grievous to self-love, and therefore most profitable to the soul. It embraces everything, and excepts nothing. 'Wherever you find yourself' it says. Measure your progress, therefore, by your fidelity to this rule; or, better still, if you can, be faithful to it without consciously reverting to it.

'Love to be unknown and esteemed as nothing' is another excellent counsel from the same source. Self-love dreads nothing so much as being unnoticed. It loves to be seen, to be known and to be thought well of. Do not allege your duty to God and men: be content to remain hidden. God will know how to find you and use you, when it is necessary for His glory and for the salvation of souls. As far as you are free to choose, avoid such positions as are likely to induce publicity and bring you to the notice of others. Then any notice will not harm you, since you are exposed to it in spite of yourself. God will make use of you, even if it means your being noticed, when you no longer run any risk, and a reputation for sanctity will not be a danger for you.

Be glad that God should appear to treat you as unknown to Him, and as of no account. Rejoice when you see others receive His consolations and favours, and you yourself only knocks and loneliness. After all, what are you: what do you deserve? And what ought you to want other than that God should deal justly with you in this world by treating you as a sinner--in fact as nothing at all!

Finally: know well that you will advance only in the measure in which you do violence to yourself. Allow no quarter, no arguing with self-love. He is a criminal, and you must hound him to death, imploring his destruction at the hands of God. 'Burn me, prune me here below' cried St. Augustine, 'if only Thou grant me mercy in eternity'. This seems terrible and frightening to nature, but in practice, it is not so bad as wethink; and it is the only way to peace and happiness. The more self-love is brought under control, the greater will be our freedom, our independence and serenity.

Let us go boldly to battle, then, against this enemy of our peace and sanctity. Let us carry our attacks to the bitter end, asking of God as a great grace that He will Himself strike the final blow. We can do a great deal to hasten the end, but only God can achieve complete victory.

106.   Cf. John ix. 41
107.   2 Cor. x. 17

Eighteenth Maxim: A retired love

Stay quietly at home: regulate your day, and waste no time.

Love of retirement and solitude disposes the soul in a special manner for the practice of the interior life. I will lead her into the wilderness, and speak to her heart. [108] When a man is alone with his own soul, undisturbed by the excitement of external things, his thoughts, unless he is beset by some violent passion, will naturally turn first to himself and then lead him back to God.

I do not mean that persons living in the world should lead a life of retirement such as is practised in convents and hermitages. Living at home, going out merely as duty requires, is living in retirement. Having no dealings with the world but such as are required by necessity or charity, is living in solitude. He who loves to be alone with God and, amid the turmoil of business, longs for the time when he may hold free converse with Him, has already, or soon will have, entered upon the interior way.

Take advantage, then, of all the leisure your affairs allow you, and reserve some part of every day for the consideration of eternal things. These are most precious moments which, if rightly used, will enable you to sanctify the remainder of your day. Another excellent practice, which draws down many graces is to put aside a week every year as a time of retreat, preferably in a religious house, spent in undisturbed meditation on the truths pertaining to salvation, in a serious examination of the state of your soul, and in a thorough and earnest preparation for the future.

Silence is one of the first-fruits of such a retreat. It is the friend of recollection and prayer, and cannot be too highly recommended. The interior spirit reigns, or soon will do, in religious houses where silence is studiously observed. Fidelity to that rule is the safeguard of all the rest; laxity and even disorder inevitably follow its neglect.

In the world, it is not so easy to have fixed times for silence, because occasions for speaking present themselves when least expected. But we observe the spirit of silence when we speak only when necessity demands, and to the point. When, in the presence of others, without affecting an ill-timed taciturnity, we prefer to listen rather than to speak; and when we have to talk keep our conversation within bounds, and observe such reticence as the Holy Spirit suggests. This reticence was one of the marks by which, according to the prophet Isaias, Our Lord was to be known. He shall not cry, nor have respect to person: neither shall his voice be heard abroad. [109] Even among devout persons, those who lead an interior life are easily recognized by this same sign. Their conversation is not less natural for that; actually it is more agreeable and interesting, and, though tempered by a certain reserve, is neither dull, cold nor constrained.

When the soul is in its first religious fervour it needs no exhortation to solitude and silence: it is naturally inclined to seek them. The loss of spiritual delights is then too much dreaded, the secret pleasure taken in them is too sweet to allow any desire for distractions from without. Intercourse with worldly persons is burdensome; it seems all a terrible void and is shunned, perhaps too much so to meet the demands of one's position, and those of Christian charity.

But there is a fault to which one is liable at this stage, and that is the tendency to share indiscreetly our innermost thoughts with those with whom we are intimate; to pour out our feelings too freely when with them, telling them of our own happiness in the hope of winning them to God. We feel unable to contain the grace that fills us, and find comfort in sharing our secret with others. But we would do better to keep it to ourselves, and mention these things only to our confessor. The inner workings of grace are not such as should be divulged. We should keep them hidden, and not aim at being apostles when we are as yet but weak beginners.

When, however, the spring-time is past, and dryness has succeeded to delight, there is reason to fear that we will give up our life of retirement and seek consolation in created things. This natural inclination must be resisted as a most dangerous temptation, which exposes the rising structure of our perfection to imminent ruin. Though we then no longer feel God's sensible presence, He is present with us in a deeper and more ineffable way, which we can easily lose if we are not extremely careful to preserve it. All voluntary distractions aim a real blow at this genuine, if unperceived, recollection. They leave impressions on the mind which are revived when we are at prayer, all the more so since the soul in times of dryness is empty of ideas and feelings. Prayer thus becomes a continual distraction, which is culpable at least in principle. And as already we have found contemplative prayer difficult, since it seemed as though God had abandoned us, we soon give it up, and with it, the interior life as well.

It is not enough, however, to stay quietly at home, keeping silence: we must also arrange our time and distribute the duties of the day, so that each duty has its appointed hour, and every hour its duty. We shall thus avoid boredom, with the inevitable temptations which follow in its train. The chief thing is to have definite hours for rising and retiring, for on that all the rest depends. Then we must distribute our devotional exercises during the day--mental prayer, Holy Mass, reading, vocal prayer, visits to the Blessed Sacrament-in such wise that some are spread over the morning, others in the evening, and there is no time of the day which is not given to God. Whatever time remains at our free disposition will be devoted to work and the duties of our state. It is as well to have our confessor's approval for all we do, but once our time-table is approved, it should be adhered to strictly.

However, as God does not want us to be slaves except to His love and holy will, which are above all external rules, and as any number of unforeseen things may cause our routine to be upset, we must adapt ourselves always to the dispositions of Divine Providence, and not reproach ourselves with exceptions for which we are not responsible. We are always faithful, if we are as faithful as we are able to be. Exactness with regard to God lies less in the fulfilling of the letter than in the disposition of the will. To break the rules of charity, propriety and courtesy in order to observe our rule of time, would be a want of fidelity to God. True piety is in no wise opposed to the fulfilment of our social duties. On the contrary, it sanctifies our relations with our neighbour, even when these seem most trifling, and are only dependent upon custom and politeness. We are not required to renounce them; indeed, we are not even allowed to neglect them

Therefore, in the first place, we must so arrange our rule that we may be able to observe it habitually, not overburdening it with practices nor multiplying them

excessively, so as to fetter the spirit and enslave the soul.
We must consider our health, our position, occupations,
and the persons on whom we depend, and to whom we owe
the greatest deference. Next, when interrupted, such as by
unforeseen business, letters or visits to be paid or received,
we must not scruple to forgo the devotional exercise
assigned to the time thus taken up, but resume it later on, if
possible. Nor must we make ourselves odious or ridiculous
by mistimed exactitude, nor show by our manner and
bearing that we are disturbed and have other things to do,
but gracefully lend ourselves not only to friends, but to
troublesome and importunate persons. God permits these
little crosses in order to break our will, give us a free and
pliable spirit, like that of St. Francis of Sales, and lead us to
the practice of many virtues which we would have no
opportunity of practising, except under such conditions.

Finally, in order to prevent all scruples, we should carefully
distinguish as to what does and does not depend upon
ourselves; what we are free to do, and what would annoy
those whom we are bound to consider. We must distinguish
such practices as preserve our liberty of spirit without in
anyway straining our fidelity, from such as encourage
constraint, pettiness and an exaggerated rigidity. If we are
honest with ourselves and with God, we can always readily
decide whether we are to blame or not for having omitted
some particular devotion.

Such arrangement of one's day as I have suggested, I
realize of course can only be observed by those who are
more or less masters of their own time. Those who are not
free to dispose of their day, if they are truly desirous of
advancing in virtue, will make use of all their free
moments, and carefully husband the time they may call
their own, in order to employ it in prayer and holy reading.

They must not complain, however, of the hardship of their position, since it is in the order of Divine Providence, and will in no way hinder their progress, if they are genuinely drawn to the interior life. God Himself will more than make up to them for their want of ordinary means, and it may be that their condition, busy and hampered as it is, will tend more to their sanctification than a state of greater leisure and independence. There are no obstacles for those who are determined to love God. Everything will become a means to loving Him, provided they have God's glory always in view, and bless His loving bounty in all He sends.

There are many reasons why a Christian should thus regulate his day, if he is able to do so. The first is that it is the bounden duty of everyone to sanctify his actions. It is already a beginning if we are able to arrange our day so that we may reasonably presume it to be in accordance with God's will, and, with that end in view, to do everything at the proper time, as though God Himself were calling us to it.

Secondly, when our devotions are thus regulated, they are less easily forgotten, and the sooner become habitual. The hour itself reminds us of the duty attached to it, and very often calls for some act of self-denial, since we may have to lay aside what we are doing in order to do what God is asking of us.

Again, we thus avoid idleness, a temptation to which those whose time is at their disposal are always exposed. We are all naturally inclined to indolence and laziness, and unless we have a clear and definite object in view, are bound to be a prey to disquietude and inconstancy in our thoughts. We commence any number of things and finish none: in short, we do not know what to do with our time, and often for want of occupation indulge in vain and even dangerous amusements. But idleness has no fears for those whose days are fully occupied. They are not left wondering what they shall do next: every hour has its appointed task, and the various duties which succeed one another do not allow the spirits to flag.

Finally, one is thereby relieved from boredom, which is undoubtedly the scourge most to be feared, and the inevitable portion of all who have no definite aim in life. It is to escape the pursuit of so inexorable an enemy that worldly folk multiply and vary indefinitely their pleasures. One would think that they sought these pleasures for the satisfaction they find in them, but it is not so. They simply use them as a remedy for their boredom, but without the least success. They are constrained to flee from it ceaselessly, but find it everywhere, and it is in vain that they make the attempt. They will always find it, for boredom pursues them relentlessly, following them wherever they take refuge. The only way to put oneself out of the reach of this torment of the so-called fortunate ones of this world is to lead a serious and planned life, in which the mind has always something definite to occupy it, and where the very variety of one's occupations serves as a relaxation.

When thus protected from idleness and boredom, how many temptations are prevented from entering the soul; how many occasions of sin avoided . From there two sources (that is, idleness and boredom) arise almost all the evils that beset society. They make men evilly inclined and unhappy. Be always occupied in conformity with the will of God and the duties of your state, and neither the passions nor the devil will have any hold over you, and you will be as virtuous and happy as it is possible to be in this life.

What I have said refers to all Christians in general, according as their circumstances permit. As to those who lead an interior life, they are more inclined to regulate their time than others, and they keep to their rules more faithfully. The spirit of God, in Whom they live and by Whom they are led, allows them no indefinite way of life, and demands a strict account of all their time. But it is not to be expected that they will always follow the one rule: they may have to vary it according to the stages through which they are passing. Practices which were useful in the beginning are not necessarily suitable later on. The spirit of God sometimes forbids what at other times it demands. Exercises proper to a retired life should occupy the early years; afterwards, God may leave them more liberty to mix in external affairs for the sake of others. There will be times when it will be necessary for them to retire within themselves; at others, they will have to yield to whatever draws them out of themselves, and helps them to forget themselves. Thus, for example during times of great distress, the director may wisely allow them such innocent pleasures or amusements as will assist them, which at another he would undoubtedly forbid. I say no more on this point, because I am not writing for advanced souls, but for beginners.

108.   Osee ii. 14
109.   Isaias xlii. 2

Nineteenth Maxim: Discretion

Let charity and piety begin at home.

Neglect of business and domestic duties under pretext of
piety is a fairly common fault. Devotees, especially of the
female sex, often fall into this error, and so give scandal
even to sensible and really religious people. Yet it is not
piety that is to blame, but rather their self-will which is
followed instead of the spirit of God.

Many have no sooner taken up the practices of religion
than they start neglecting their homes, their children, and
those dependent upon them. They spend the day going to
church, in running after popular preachers, attending every
religious service and special festival, and in undertaking all
manner of good works. They are to be found everywhere
except at home, which they leave as early, and return to as
late, as possible.

Meanwhile, all is disorder in the household; everyone does
as he pleases in the absence of the mistress. Children are
left to the doubtful care of those who themselves want
looking after; or they are dragged about, especially if girls,
from service to service, until they are wearied out and
disgusted, and soon begin to tire of religion. The husband
very rightly complains, but his word is not heeded, and he
is secretly accused of not being sufficiently devout.

And thus it is, too, with many men. They are active,
bustling busybodies; meddling in everything under the
pretext of serving God; fancying that the Church depends
on them. They concern themselves with the affairs of
others, and neglect their own. Even some priests are not
entirely exempt from these and similar faults. They are

zealous, but, as St. Paul says, not according to knowledge. [110] They allow their natural activity full rein, and because their ministry is spread over many objects insinuate themselves into everything and imagine that all good works must pass through their hands, otherwise they will not succeed. They are for ever coming and going, and the day is not long enough for all they have to do. They even borrow from the night, and leave themselves barely time to say their office.

I am not saying this in a spirit of criticism: nothing is further from my wish. But how can I do otherwise than lament over such an evil as this, which is so harmful to the cause of religion? I am not calling into question the intention: that I well believe to be right and good. Nor do I blame the objects in view, which are also good, since they concern the worship of God and the welfare of men. But how can one rejoice to see the order of duty reversed, and works of supererogation take precedence over duties of obligation? Who can excuse that mistaken piety which looks merely to externals, counts the inner spirit as nothing, and neglects God's primary laws?

The spirit of the inner life follows quite another course, and inspires ideas the very opposite of what I have been describing. It teaches all who yield to its guidance that their first duty is the sanctification of their own souls, and that Christian sanctity consists primarily in the fulfilment of the duties of one's state. These are indispensable. The very end of devotion is the obtaining of such graces as are necessary for their fulfilment, and it can never, therefore, be a reason for neglecting them. On the contrary, true piety allows such time only for prayer as can lawfully be spared from duties of obligation. In all religious exercises not of strict obligation, it bids us accommodate ourselves to the wishes and frailties of those whom we are bound to consider, and, for the sake of peace, to sacrifice our own tastes, be they never so pious.

The inward spirit also reminds us that we must only undertake good works such as are left to our discretion, in so far as they do not encroach on our spirit of recollection. Should they even begin to make inroads thereon and dissipate us ever so little, we must absolutely give them up, or put them off until another time when we shall not run the same risk. In all such circumstances, it is best not to act on our own but take sound advice before acting, or wait until God sends the occasion. We must also be on our guard against our natural activity and ardour, and all indiscreet zeal which would have us take on far more than we can manage, so that there remains no time for prayer, and for the duties of our state, which are always the first of all good works.

The true interior spirit also teaches those who are charged with the sacred ministry that the care of souls should be limited to spiritual matters, and only extended to temporal things when charity requires it of them, and then with much reserve and circumspection, lest these should prove harmful to themselves or lessen in the minds of others the reverence due to their sacred office.

Such has ever been the mind of the Church from earliest times. The apostles were the first to set an example in this matter by appointing deacons to see to the needs of the poor, reserving to themselves the duty of prayer and the ministry of the word. [111] In whatever time remains over from the administration of the sacraments, from preaching, the direction of souls, visiting the sick and other similar duties, the primary duty of priests should be prayer, the reading of sacred books and other studies proper to their state. They ought to concern themselves in temporal affairs only in so far as they are a matter of conscience, by pointing out the rules which should be followed so as not to offend against justice or charity, and to maintain or reestablish unity and peace. In the matter of good works or works of mercy, they should, if possible, confine themselves to directing affairs, committing the carrying out of them to those well qualified to do so. Otherwise, apart from losing time, they will lay themselves open to complaints, murmurings, and sometimes unworthy suspicions. The closer they live in intimate union with God, the better will they serve the cause of religion and procure the salvation of souls, the greater authority and consideration will they possess, and their reputation will remain intact and their good name respected.

All this would be taught by the spirit of the interior life, if men sought its guidance with a pure intention. Thus it taught St. Ambrose, St. Augustine, St. John Chrysostom, St. Charles Borromeo, St. Francis of Sales, and every other saint and doctor of the Church throughout the ages, and those most zealous for the greater glory of God and the good of souls.

110.   Cf. Rom. x. 2
111.   Acts vi. 2-4

Twentieth Maxim: Social relationships

Be cordial and kind, gentle and lowly; considerate towards others, severe upon yourself.

What a number of precepts, what a wealth of detail is contained in this maxim.

To begin with, virtue is not virtue unless it is lovable: where it is not, it is imperfect. And its imperfection is due to self-love and self-esteem. When humility has dried up these two sources of all our shortcomings and evil habits, then virtue reveals itself in all its loveliness, and men cannot help but pay it homage, even though they may not show it. For virtue causes us to render to others the feelings we entertain for ourselves, so that what would be unwarrantable self-love in our own case becomes praiseworthy charity when directed towards others. It leads us to do to others as we would be done by; to think and speak, and even suffer from them, as we would have them act in our regard. Certainly no one could refuse the tribute of his love for such a virtue when he sees it in others, and all men would love one another if they were virtuous.

True piety, therefore, will inspire in the true servant of God all that will make him lovable, and its first sign is gentleness. If he is austere, it is only towards himself, and even then only in the measure of a holy discretion. Towards others, he is kind, easy and accommodating, in so far as his conscience permits. If at times he is obliged to be severe, charity is always the principle of his severity. He is never forbidding or rude, but always approachable and friendly. When we decide to live devoutly in the world, it would be a mistake to break off all social intercourse and lead too secluded a life, in order to give ourselves up wholly to pious exercises. Because we have given ourselves to God, that does, mean that we are to have no more friends (assuming, of course, that such friendships are not dangerous or will not dissipate us in any way). There is no need to deprive ourselves of the pleasure of their society. Visits of courtesy--even those which would appear to be purposeless and tiresome--need not be a burden to us. What would the world think of a pious person who shut himself up in his home and refused to see anybody; or, if he must see them, presented a cold and forbidding countenance? By withdrawing thus from all social intercourse, he would render piety odious, and give the impression that it was most unreasonable. It would also deprive him of many opportunities for practising virtue, and he would contract the very faults and form a habit of mind which true religion condemns.

Undoubtedly it is good to have a fixed time for one's religious duties and, so far as possible, to discharge them faithfully. But we should not multiply them to such an extent that they effect our whole day, and leave us no time to give to our fellow creatures. Besides, charity always knows how to adapt and even sacrifice itself in the matter of devotions, in accordance with the consideration it owes to others.

True piety, further, evinces much gentleness in the exercise of authority, especially towards children and other dependents. It is never rigid, unyielding and exacting. When it rebukes, it does so without undue severity. It readily forgives, and does not search for every tiny fault. Threats are never on its lips, nor chastisement in its hand. Above all, it avoids outbursts of impatience and temper, hard words and reproaches, all that mortifies and hurts without helping to correct. It ever seeks to make others good, but not in a harsh way, and it does not expect perfection to be reached in a day. It waits patiently, and returns again and again to the same point. It consoles, encourages, has a good word for good will, and praises the smallest efforts in order to induce greater.

But the especial fault which it is the object of true piety to correct in us is irritability or moodiness. Everyone understands the term, but it is not easy to define it. It is laid to the charge of devout persons more than to any others. Mistaken piety often gives occasions for its display. The cross humour to which I allude does not arise from malice; it is not a failing of bad people, but on the contrary of the frank and straightforward. But it causes many heart-aches of which one is veritably ashamed when the fit has passed, and it is intolerable in the presence of others. Politeness teaches us to check it amongst strangers and those we respect, but we are not so quick to repress it among friends or at home. And those who give way to it are the first to suffer from its effects.

Nothing is more difficult to extirpate than this moodiness, because it is not excited for any particular reason, nor by any recognized moral cause; it depends in great measure on physical causes. What is more, it forestalls any kind of reflection on our part, and its fits come on when least expected. What hold can the will have on such a complaint, once middle-age has been reached? I know of but one remedy and that is the practice of the presence of God and of contemplative prayer. The first warns us of any stirrings of bad temper and checks them; the second gradually establishes the soul in a state of calm, keeps the imagination within bounds, modifies sensitiveness, and puts to flight low spirits, which are, I should say, the chief source of ill humour.

But the gentleness inspired by virtue must not be confused with that mildness which is purely natural. Those who are meek by nature are often weak, soft, indifferent, apathetic and unduly indulgent. Those, on the contrary, whose gentleness is an acquired virtue, are strong and firm. Their feelings run deep and are affected equally by good and evil. They are indulgent when it is advisable to be so, but never if it involves breaking the rules of duty. Those who are naturally meek are afraid to reprove lest they become excited and upset, while those who are virtuously gentle reprove strongly and even vigorously, but always with selfpossession. The former dissemble through timidity, the others speak according to the promptings of charity. The former often run the risk of failing in their duty on some point, the latter will always fulfil their duty faithfully, without human respect. The former spare others in order to spare themselves, the latter only for God's greater glory, and as a duty of the highest order. As to that gentleness which is merely scheming, it is a vice which all agree in condemning.

Cordiality is another outcome of true piety. It was long ago banished from ordinary social intercourse, and its place taken by politeness, which resembles it externally, but dissimulates its feelings, affecting those it does not possess and hiding those it does. These demonstrations are received and paid back in the same coin, but in reality no reliance is to be placed on them, and they deceive no one with the least experience. The first lesson taught by the world to its votaries is to appear candid, but never to be cordial. And the word itself is almost as little used in modern- day speech as the thing itself is rare in society. Polite intercourse is reduced to vain and frequently contemptuous compliments, to offers of service the acceptance of which would be annoying, unmeaning promises easily to be evaded at the time of fulfilment, assurances of good will which always end in declarations of regret, and demonstrations of interest in other's concerns that appear to be genuine but are in reality often cold and completely false.

How different is this outward affectation from real Christian cordiality. Charity never fails in the requirements of true courtesy, but with them combines frankness and candour. It expresses only what it feels, and that simply, unaffectedly and persuasively. There is no evasion, no reticence, no affectation, all comes from the heart. It is love that prompts speech, discretion that holds it in check. Sweet and safe and satisfactory are the relations with minds inspired by charity. The first Christians, we are told, had but one heart and one soul, [112] for they looked upon themselves as members of one body joined to one Head.

This is the divine unity that Our Lord asked of His Father on the night of His Passion. Father, He prayed, that they all may be one, as Thou in Me and I in Thee; that they also may be one in Us; that the world may believe that Thou hast sent Me. [113] By that sign Our Lord wills that the divine origin of His religion should be known. If only that unity reigned on earth, happiness would reign likewise. It was Our Lord's mind that it should begin in this world and be consummated eternally in heaven. But where is it today? In the hearts of a very small number of Christians, far fewer than is generally supposed. The hearts of the rest are crossed by a thousand petty views of self-interest and self-seeking, which, though they may not kill it, render charity cold and constrained.

Kindliness adds to cordiality a certain disposition which takes all in good part, puts the best construction on things, is not quick to take offence, and is neither captious nor suspicious: a quality not usually found among devout persons. These are so apt to judge others severely, because they are able to recognize good and evil, and have greater lights by which they discern these things in others.

Another fault which is fairly common in such persons is that of esteeming oneself better than everyone else. Self-esteem and spiritual vanity are among the most dangerous snares which beset anyone new to the interior life. No sooner have we given ourselves to God and think we perceive a noticeable improvement in our behaviour, than we begin to make comparisons. How superior we are and, thank God, how free from the defects we notice in others! And so it goes on, and before we know where we are, we repeat the words of the Pharisee in the Gospel: O God, I give Thee thanks that I am not as the rest of men. [114]

These feelings are generally enhanced if one has felt a certain sensible sweetness at communion. If emotion has wrung from us a few tears, at once the soul fancies that it is lifted up right above this world and given eagles' wings for the loftiest of flights. This is a subtle temptation which it is difficult altogether to avoid, unless God gives a helping hand or withdraws His misused consolations. Spiritual pride is unquestionably more to be feared than any other, since its objects are so much more excellent. Wherefore, God allows those who yield to it to be visited with still greater blindness, and its victims are exposed to the danger of their eternal loss.

Those directors who have not the spirit of God are equally apt to presume on their gifts, and fancy themselves more enlightened than others. They persuade themselves that they have a special gift for the guidance of souls, and that others know nothing about it. They are proud of the number and quality of their penitents, and use secret devices to increase their number. If they are not continually boasting of their own powers, that work is done for them by other lips. They express pity for those who apply to other priests and imply that it is a matter for regret that persons so well disposed should not have fallen into better hands. Their first business, therefore, when someone submits to their direction, is to destroy the work that has been done by others and to suggest new methods, insisting that their penitents should adopt an altogether different way of life. Directors of this kind have an intensely domineering spirit, and exercise despotic sway over souls. They do not bring them into subjection to grace but to their own notions. They never tell them to listen to the voice of God speaking in their hearts: no, God is supposed to speak through their instrumentality alone, and any inward inspiration not in accordance with their views is treated as an illusion. I pray you, devout souls, avoid these despots, and seek such as will watch the work of grace in your soul, and conform their advice to the guidance of the Holy Spirit. Their one lesson will be to teach you to be attentive and docile to the voice of the Good Shepherd.

To overlook the faults of others is a fundamental rule of Christian charity; severity with our own the first principle of interior mortification. But many who profess to be interior souls assume just the opposite. There has always been, and always will be, ground for complaint on this score.

How easy is that devotion which consists in blaming and criticizing other people, sometimes with intolerable harshness, sometimes with an affectation of pity. Where is the charity in a person who will not bear with others, but turns to ridicule all that he disapproves, either with or without reason; who makes no allowance for anything, not even for human frailty? We are not obliged to flatter our neighbour in spite of his reprehensible characteristics, but we should bear with him, and not let him see that his company is not agreeable to us. With whom are we to live if we only live with those who are faultless? By what rule of equity would you have others, not only put up with you but take pleasure in your company and adapt themselves to your peculiarities, when you are not prepared to bear their burdens, which are quite as heavy as your own? Are you yourself faultless? And yet you feel that others should make allowances for you. At least, then, be indulgent towards them. Of all defects, intolerance towards others is the most disgraceful. Bear ye one another's burdens, and so you shall fulfil the law of Christ. [115] So says St. Paul, and he comes back to the same thing in almost all his epistles. It is, indeed, a most important factor in life, most necessary for the common good, and it helps to make things run smoothly. The natural law has even endowed it with the force of a precept, so essential is it in its eyes. An ancient poet insisted that, just as love is blind to the defects in the object of its affections, so should we be to the shortcomings of our friends; that we should disguise them under favourable terms, even as a father hides the corporal blemishes of his son. The apostle would have Christians love one another with the same kind of love, and encourage the same kind of union, as members of a body. [116] The members of the human body, he seems to say, do more than support one another. They come to one another's aid as need arises, and watch with assiduous care in the conservation of the whole, the stronger coming to the aid of the weaker members. So St. Paul would have us act in like manner, one towards another, as members of one body.

Take the example of Our Lord Himself, and consider how
He lived with His apostles. He was holiness itself, they
coarse and far from perfect. What could He see in them that
provoked His love; and what did He not see that did not
repel it? It would seem that the holier He was, the more
painful it must have been to live with them; He might have
been excused if He had had less indulgence towards them,
and yet it was just the contrary. Never was a master more
compassionate, more condescending. With what kindness
He taught them, adapting His teaching to their lack of
understanding, repeating His lessons, emphasizing them,
explaining in private what He had said in public. With what
gentleness He reprimanded them for their jealousy, their
ambition, for their quarrels amongst themselves. Their
failure to grasp the heavenly meaning of all He said, their
Jewish prejudices, their misguided opinion of His Person--
none of these things shocked Him. Indeed, He preferred
their ignorant simplicity to the knowledge of the doctors,
and to the proud justice of the Pharisees, who found no
greater fault in Him than that He associated with the lowly,
especially with sinners. See how wonderfully He spoke to
the disciples in His discourse after the Last Supper.

And St. Paul, the perfect imitator of Christ, made himself
all things to all men, in order that he might win the world to
Christ. Not that he sought to please men; his thoughts were
far higher than that. But he bent down to them so that he
might raise them up to him. He made their miseries his
own, so touched was he by their need. He tells Christians
that they must rejoice with those that rejoice, and weep
with those that weep. [117] Who is weak, he said, and I am
not weak; who is scandalized, and I am not on fire? [118]
He wanted the strong to help the weak; that they should not
seek their own pleasure, but be to one another what Jesus
was to them.

St. John, the beloved disciple, would seem to reduce the whole of his teaching to the love of one's neighbour, and to that charity which endures all. In his extreme old age, no longer able to preach long discourses, he contented himself with repeating the simple words: Little children, love one another. [119] And when it was complained that he always said the same thing, he replied in effect that such was the commandment of the Lord, and it alone was enough, provided one fulfilled it.

Now of all the duties contained in this precept the most essential is the patient endurance of one's neighbour, because it calls for sustained effort and its results are of the greatest consequence, whether the commandment be kept or no. It is also the most difficult, since it demands continuous vigilance, and unremitting efforts to overcome ourselves. To bear all from others, giving them no occasion to bear anything from us, is a sign of very great virtue.

But to arrive at this state, what a deadly war must be waged with our personal defects, with that self-love which is at the root of them. Say what we will, the true reason that makes us so fastidious in regard to others is our own excessive self-love and self-esteem. The more we spare ourselves, the less do we consider others. The blinder we are to our own imperfections, the clearer do we perceive the defects of others. The great and only way to become charitable is to give oneself wholeheartedly to the practice of interior mortification, to apply the knife and cautery to our own wounds, and to uproot down to the tiniest fibre our secret self-complacency. Rest assured that in the measure in which selflove dies in us, will the love of our neighbour grow.

But that is just what men will not listen to. Of all the forms of mortification, interior mortification is the most distasteful to nature. Men will willingly overburden themselves with austerities, regretting those they cannot undertake; they will fast beyond their strength, undertake all manner of devotional practices, spend hours of the day in prayer: but break their will, repress their bad temper, try to overcome their sensitiveness, check their unfounded suspicions, their malicious curiosity, their rash judgments and unjust prejudices; in a word, make war on all the vices of the heart and mind--this few are prepared to do, so painful is it to nature. And fewer still have the courage to carry it to a successful issue.

112.   Acts iv. 32
113.   John xvii. 21
114.   Luke xviii. 11
115.   Gal. vi. 2
116.   Cf. I Cor. xii. 27
117.   Rom. xii. 15
118.   2 Cor. xi. 29
119.   Cf. I John iv. 7

Twenty-first Maxim: Progress

Go straight on: never stop or look back. Grieve for sin, but never lose courage.

It is not enough to enter upon the ways of God: we must walk in them, and ever press forward. To refuse to go on is to consent to fall back, for in this matter it is impossible to stand still for long. In the interior way to which God introduces us, it is He also Who regulates our speed, causing some to advance more rapidly, others more slowly. Our part is never to resist the hand that is urging us on, and to do nothing to retard our progress.

Now this progress is retarded, or arrested altogether, in various ways and for various reasons, which it would be as well to explain. It is retarded by cowardice, faint-heartedness, infidelity, inconstancy, and by a great number of tiny faults into which we fall, either for want of vigilance over ourselves, or of attention to what God is telling us in the depths of our heart.

Our progress is arrested when, like a careless traveller, we look to right and left, and stop to examine the things we see. Note, I do not say that we go out of our way to seek these objects: that would be far graver, especially if, in order to enjoy them, we gave up altogether. I am assuming we keep to the path and intend to do so; but, fascinated by the beauty and novelty of all that is around us, we slacken pace, or stop to enjoy it at our leisure. For to look at these things in a vague and superficial manner need not hold us up, provided the attraction does not become too strong.

We do much the same when we are perpetually looking to see where to put our feet, always trying to choose the best places, and making any number of detours to avoid awkward spots, instead of walking straight on and risking getting our feet wet! Nothing is more common in following the interior way than these precautions, hesitations and deliberations. We want to be quite sure before risking a false step. We want to see where we are going. We are afraid of over-tiring ourselves, and so turn aside from difficult and slippery places, or where there is the slightest appearance of danger. But grace tells us not to be afraid, to go straight ahead. Otherwise the way will only be all the longer, and we may never reach the end. Any kind of oversensitiveness, faint-heartedness, an exaggerated fear of falling or of soiling, ever so little, our conscience (which can be a form of pride): all this is a hindrance to grace, and prevents us from pressing on unhesitatingly with full confidence in God, without watching our every step and making long detours.

In a path so rough and uneven, with difficult places everywhere and precipices on either side, why should we be so afraid of falls and of the danger of sullying ourselves, when we ought to walk blindly under the safe conduct of faith; when such falls can only be slight and involuntary and only have the effect of keeping us humble; when God's hand is always ready toraise us up again? The fear of death or of wounds never made a good soldier. We have a Physician Who can and will heal us and give us new life. Why, then, need we so greatly fear to expose ourselves by His orders, and under His all-powerful protection?

Again, we stop when, having accidentally fallen, instead of getting up again immediately and continuing with renewed energy, we lie on the ground distressed, miserable and despondent, and make no effort to get up. Or, if we do get up, we stop to investigate the cause of our fall, under the pretext of guarding against a similar accident in future. All this kind of conduct implies much self-love, false discretion, and self-confidence.

He who walks rapidly--or, better still, he who runs --is not so careful to see where he sets his feet. He overcomes all obstacles, and presses on steadily whether his path be impeded with ruts or mire, or is overflowing with water. What does it matter to him, if he is splashed, muddy and wet, provided he is making progress? He is willing to expose himself to a few falls, in spite of which he leaves others far behind. These accidents, which he neither seeks nor fears, and are only caused by the eagerness of his efforts, have no bad consequences. On the contrary, they increase his ardour. He gets up again promptly and thinks no more about it. God, towards Whom he is making his way, and union with Whom he is so eagerly seeking, is too merciful and just to lay to his account those faults, which are occasioned by an excess of confidence in Him, of abandonment and of love.

All this, however, is to be understood only of those souls that are truly interior, of whom God has taken full possession, who are acted upon and led by His Spirit, according to the expression of St. Paul. [120] Who have a horror of the tiniest deliberate fault, and of the least resistance to grace; who, moreover, have great courage and are determined to spare no sacrifice. But it would be wrong to apply this doctrine to ordinary souls who, aided by grace, advance more by their own efforts in the path of virtue. These must always use prudent, though not anxious, circumspection; watch carefully their steps, and be on their guard against all falls, the more so because their falls are generally wilful, either in fact or in principle.

But, it will be said, how can we be sure that we are advancing? The answer is that we must look for no such assurance. It is enough to know that we are not halting on the way, and this we know by the witness of a quiet conscience, or from an habitual though not necessarily conscious peace. In times of perplexity and darkness, this assurance is conveyed to us by our spiritual director, who tells us that all is well; who soothes us and bids us plod on steadily, relying solely on faith and obedience.

I allow that faith is dark, and obedience blind: that the assurance derived from them does not do away with the contrary impressions produced by the imagination and feeling. I grant that this assurance is to a certain extent obscure, and that it brings with it no comforting conviction on which the soul can rest. But it is the kind of assurance that suits the trial, and so long as the trial lasts no other must be expected, unless occasionally and momentarily.

What difficulty would there be in this way if the soul were always certain that it was pleasing in God's sight? Where would be the sacrifice? What proof would the soul give of its trust and self- abandonment? Had Abraham known beforehand that God's command to immolate Isaac was only a test, and that an angel would stay his arm at the very moment it was about to strike, where would have been the merit, and what glory would he have given to God? And the same with Isaac: if, as he lay bound for the sacrifice, he had known that he was not going to die? Such an immolation would only have been a feigned one.

So, then, continual progress means that we must go straight ahead, urged on by grace and directed by obedience, knowing neither the road we tread nor the end to which it is leading us; unconscious whether our actions are pleasing to

God and will meet with reward or no. We must wilfully think of none of these things, but simply be absorbed by the consideration of God's good pleasure and will, which we are sure of fulfilling provided we do not fulfil our own.

But what is to be done when, instead of advancing we seem to be falling back? In this matter, we must not be guided by our own judgment, because there comes a time in the spiritual life when the soul does not know its own state, and must not know it. This is the time when we imagine we are yielding to temptation. We think we are cast off by God by reason of our sins; we imagine we see sin in all we do. Are we therefore falling back? Far from it: we were never advancing more surely. It is then we act with greater purity of intention, seeing that we are seeking self in nothing, nor our interests, either in creatures or from God. It is then that self-love, reduced to its last resources, receives its fatal blows, and it is then that we give God the sacrifice that glorifies Him most.

That does not mean, however, that we are aware of our progress. Every step seems to warn us that we are heading for the loss of everything. And in a sense we do lose ourselves, but only to find ourselves eternally in God. Oh infinitely happy loss, which could never take place if we knew beforehand how it would all end. And so the experienced director is careful not to give the soul any assurance of its safety merely to console it. He emboldens it to continue sacrificing itself, but he does not unveil the mystery of what that sacrifice is leading to, nor reveal the exceeding happiness which will ensue for the faithful soul. Were he to act otherwise, he would hinder the work of God, and the consummation of the holocaust.

That is also why, when this point is reached, God takes every precaution so that nothing shall spoil His work. Maybe He will withdraw the director and send another, who understands nothing of the state of that soul. Or, if He keeps him, He will seal his lips completely, and prevent him from giving any illtimed consolation. He may even permit him to turn against the soul, be prejudiced against it, and condemn it, and thus himself immolate the victim. These ineffable secrets of grace are known only to those who have experienced them, or are enlightened by God for the direction of others.

But let us return to our maxim. It forbids us to look back. We look back, when we regret what we have left behind for God's sake, even as the Israelites in the desert regretted the flesh-pots of Egypt, and loathed the manna which fell from heaven. It was in this sense that Our Lord declared that no man putting his hand to the plough and looking back is fit for the kingdom of God. [121] Even among men, regret for or the resumption of a gift once given is looked upon as contemptible, and at the most is forgiven only in a child, that does not know what it is doing.

We look back when we retrace our steps in thought and recall the past, in order out of curiosity to discern the course of our religious life and the workings of grace. This is what St. Paul condemned when, speaking of himself, he said: One thing I do: forgetting the things that are behind and stretching forth myself to those that are before, I press towards the mark, to the prize of the supernal vocation of God in Christ Jesus. [122]

We look back, when we are so attached to the various means of perfection that we cling to them obstinately, or regret them inordinately when it pleases God to deprive us of them; when we cast longing eyes on some past state, preferring it to our present condition, in which nature has more to endure.

Again we look back, when we are continually turning our head to see whether we are making any progress, and how much. For, as we cannot see the goal ahead of us, the only way in which we can judge of our progress is by looking back to our starting-point. It is self-love that inspires this curiosity, but it does not really tell us anything, and it is nearly always followed by vain complacency, or else by despondency. The only effect of these judgments and retrospections is to slacken our pace and sometimes to hold up our progress, if indeed they do not cause us to turn back altogether.

Many souls are subject to this fault. They want their director to tell them again and again that they are going on well, and that he is pleased with the progress they are making. It is to fortify them, they say, and to urge them on to yet greater efforts: but it is all an illusion. Let them leave it to their director to enlighten them when he sees fit; for there are times when he should do so, in order to keep up their courage. But, generally speaking, they would do better to remain at peace, and take it that all is well unless they are told to the contrary.

Another fault, no less common and equally connected with self- love, is to be anxious and distressed at the slightest fault that escapes us, or at the least sign of our wretchedness and frailty. It is a great secret in the spiritual life to know how to meet the everyday faults that one commits, and how to turn them to good account. Let us consider this for a moment.

First of all, I assume that one has taken a firm resolution never to commit a deliberate sin, however small. Anything short of this appears to me completely incompatible with sincere devotion. By deliberate sins, I mean those one commits habitually, with full knowledge and consent, with no intention of correcting them, no contrition for them, and stifling any remorse that grace excites in the soul. I am speaking now of venial sins or simple infidelities to grace. Now the first thing God puts into the hearts of those He calls to the interior life, is a firm determination to follow in all things the inspirations of grace, and never wilfully to act against one's conscience. Thus these souls very rarely commit such faults, for if they did so frequently, they would soon fall from the state in which God has placed them.

The faults, then, to which they are subject are passing things, savouring of faint-heartedness, human respect, vanity or curiosity. Or else they are faults due to a lively nature; faults of inadvertence, indiscretion, peevishness or impulse--all imperfections of nature rather than definite faults.

The first counsel given on this subject by masters of the spiritual life is never to lose courage, whatever fault may have been committed, because discouragement arises solely from self- love. We are surprised at having fallen. We did not think we were capable of such a thing. As if a human being who is nothing but corruption, weakness and wickedness, ought to be surprised at his own lapses. Astonishment implies a hidden vexation, despondency, and a temptation to give up everything. Saints are humbled by their faults, but never discouraged; they are not surprised! They rather wonder that they commit no worse, knowing themselves to be what they are, and they are continually thanking God that His goodness has preserved them so far.

We partly cause this discouragement ourselves by allowing our imagination to brood over the fault committed. We magnify and exaggerate it, and make mountains out of molehills. The devil also intervenes in order to break down our courage and induce us to miss our communions, and generally cause us to worry.

To obviate the work of the imagination and its consequences, the second counsel is to be sorry immediately on becoming aware of a fault, and then to think no more about it, until (if necessary) the time of confession. There are some persons who imagine that they should be always thinking of their sins; they carry them about with them, and have them constantly before their eyes. Such continual remembrance of our faults is only calculated to weaken and sadden us, and prevent us from carrying out our duties. We grow scrupulous, and are always worrying our confessor.

The third counsel--and it is that of St. Francis of Sales--is to grieve for our faults for God's sake, for it is He Who is offended by them, and to rejoice over them for our own, because of the humiliation they cause us. To practise this counsel, which is one of great perfection, is to draw from our falls all the profit which God had in view in permitting them. In God's plan our daily faults are, so to speak, one of the elements which go to make up our sanctity. When He wishes, God knows how to employ for that end the greatest crimes and disorders, as He did in the case of David, Mary Magdalen, Mary the Egyptian, and many other well-known penitents. And why should not our daily faults, if only we will use them to increase our self-knowledge (the most necessary next to the knowledge of God), produce the same results? But we will discuss this somewhat more fully in our next chapter.

120.   Rom. viii. 14
121.   Luke ix. 62
122.   Phil. iii. 13-14.

Twenty-second Maxim: Dependence on grace

When we know our own helplessness, we learn to
appreciate the value and efficacy of grace.

God's first aim in our sanctification is His own glory.
Although He commands us to do all that depends on us, He
would have us acknowledge that we can do nothing of
ourselves; that our efforts are vain and our best resolutions
profitless, except His grace precedes and follows all our
good works; that it is useless to attempt to build the temple
of our sanctity unless He begins, continues and completes
the work, with our cooperation. Moreover- and this is St.
Paul's express teaching--we cannot produce a single good
thought or entertain a single good desire of ourselves.1 We
do not even know what sanctity is, or how to attain it.
These are the truths of faith so clearly set out in Scripture
and confirmed by Holy Church, and so well defended by St
Augustine against the Pelagians.

God is jealous of His glory, and He is resolved that all
sincere Christians shall learn these truths from their own
experience. By these means they acquire humility, the
mother of all the other virtues, without which those very
virtues, being infected with pride, would but add to their
condemnation. I say these things are to be learned by
experience, for what would it avail us from a practical
point of view, to know that they are truths of faith, if we
had not that intimate assurance which only experience can
give? And what would humility be, were it not rooted in a
deep conviction of the soul, arising from a continual
consciousness of its own spiritual misery?

God's dealings in this respect assume a more specially
defined form with regard to those who are in the passive

state. Of these, He takes particular care, and is the more jealous for them, since they belong to Him by their unreserved donation and consecration. As He leads them by the direct inspiration of His Spirit, and Himself assumes the task of their sanctification, bestowing greater graces on them than on others, so He takes all the more care to convince them that they are nothing and can do nothing, and that it is He Who provides for everything, and is responsible for all the good in them, and that all He requires of them is their abandonment and obedience.

But how does He lead them to that sense of absolute and total powerlessness and that perfect dependence upon grace? In the first place, He takes possession of their faculties, and does not allow them their free use in spiritual matters. They feel, as it were, bound and unable to exercise their memory, understanding and will on any particular subject. He allows them to make no plans, and should they conceive any designs otherwise than through His inspiration, He may upset them in part or altogether. He takes from them every method and practice of their own choosing. He withdraws them from ordinary efforts and from the usual means of acquiring any particular virtue. Instead, He Himself takes over the task of directing and sanctifying them according to His plan, prescribing in due measure what they are to do and what they are to avoid, infusing into their souls the habit of the virtues, so that they cannot flatter themselves that they have in any way acquired them through their own efforts. They do not even know that they possess such virtues, though in fact they practise them in such circumstances and by such means as He pleases. This state is excessively painful and humiliating to nature, most mortifying to self-love, and demands on the part of those who pass through it such

fidelity as can only be maintained by great love and
unremitting courage.

Secondly, He humbles them by the faults into which He
allows them to fall, particularly when He sees them relying
on themselves or when they have made good resolutions on
which they depend. These faults, indeed, are merely faults
of frailty, but it is precisely their own weakness that He
wants to make them conscious of. He acts like a mother
who purposely leaves her child to himself and lets him fall
without harming himself, so that he may understand his
need of her, and learn to cling closely to her, since he
cannot take a step alone without falling, nor rise again
alone after a fall.

These faults of pure frailty become more frequent, and
apparently more grave, in proportion to the progress made.
Some particular fault, which appeared to have been cured,
now seems more imperious than ever. Passions which one
thought had been mastered and brought under control,
become more rebellious. The good which I will I do not,
but the evil which I will not, that I do... For I am delighted
with the law of God according to the inward man; but I see
another law in my members, fighting against the law of my
mind, and captivating me in the law of sin. [123] After so
many favours received from God, after so many
protestations made to Him, this condition arouses deep
shame in the soul that finds itself a prey to such misery, and
it despairs of ever being able to conquer or correct itself.

In this sharp internal war between the old and the new man,
in which the latter is apparently worsted, the soul is fain to
cry: Unhappy man that I am: who shall deliver me from the
body of this death? [124] By 'this death' the soul
understands this present life, which causes it a torture

worse than death, and which it takes to be continually threatening the life of grace. All the violence I have used against myself, all my prayers, fastings, vigils and austerities, have proved of no avail against my enemy. I can do nothing more. Who, then, will deliver me? The grace of God by Jesus Christ, Our Lord, answers St. Paul. [125] Grace alone can work so great a miracle.

To this confession of the power of grace and the helplessness of the human will, it is God's intention to reduce the soul. It is His will that our deliverance by Him shall be acknowledged as a free gift, with which the soul has nothing to do except await it patiently. Thus God glorifies Himself in such a soul, leaving it no support from its own strength, and, by the consciousness of its sufferings and its vain attempts to rid itself of them, obliges it to acknowledge that its cure is due solely to the heavenly Physician.

Let us enter, then, into God's plans for us, so that our faults, our temptations, and the sense of our wretchedness, may all turn to His glory, by the humiliation they bring us, by the recognition of our powerlessness, and by an entire confidence in His divine goodness. We will grieve but not despond. Sorrow comes from God, despondency from selflove. We will humble ourselves patiently, quietly and gently. We will despair of ourselves, but expect everything from God. He will come and help us, but not until, weary, exhausted and convinced of the futility of all else, we turn to Him.

The ordinary run of Christians appreciate the value of grace, but as they add to it their own endeavours and God blesses their efforts, they do not realize its full value. In like manner, when they commit any fault, they are humbled. At the same time, they are aware that it was in their power to resist; they remind themselves that they did put up a fight before giving in. Therefore their falls are really voluntary, and they see that it depends upon themselves to rise, and that grace urges them to do so. They see also that they do not heed, because they will not heed; consequently, they have not a perfect knowledge of their own weakness. How should they, when they are always conscious of their strength, even in their very falls which they know they could have avoided. Such are those who have the free use of their faculties.

It is not so, however, with interior souls when they have entered the passive way. These are just like children, and God allows them no feeling save that of their own weakness. They are strong, but only in His strength. It must be remembered however, that this stage is only reached after their own strength has been spent in all manner of exercises, interior and exterior; for it would be a great illusion to imagine that God shows the slightest favour to laziness, indolence or want of effort. In this state of childhood, if they do any good, grace so acts in them that they are not conscious of any effort on their part, for they are deprived of all natural activity. They do cooperate, but with a cooperation which is barely perceptible, and which lies in their having given up their free will to God, to dispose of as He wishes. They are borne onwards in the way of perfection as a child is carried in its mother's arms, but not till they have of their own will thrown themselves into the arms of God, and refuse to leave them. According to the simile used by St. Teresa, they do not use sails and oars as others do; they trust to the wind to fill their sails, and it is the wind which drives them on. Now when we row, we contribute appreciably to our progress and have the right to take some credit to ourselves; but when we are carried on by the wind, we have no doubt where the strength comes from. So, in the passive state, the full value and efficacy of grace is more truly appreciated.

Souls in this state have likewise a keener and deeper consciousness of their weakness through the faults to which they give way, since it is because of their weakness that they fall. They do not want to commit such faults. Indeed, they make the most earnest resolutions against them; they multiply their prayers and austerities, and yet they fall. But God only allows this to happen, in order to keep them humble and make them realize their own nothingness. Let me repeat: I am not speaking of big faults. A soul would have to have already withdrawn itself from the grace of the passive state to fall into such sins. So long as they strive faithfully to abandon themselves to God's guiding Providence; so long as they do not intentionally permit themselves the slightest imperfection and relax no exercise of piety, their falls will not be considerable in themselves. They are exterior and apparent only, for the will has no share in them. Like St. Paul, they will be able to say: It is no more I that do it, but sin that dwelleth in me. [126] And that root of sin, which they endeavour unsuccessfully to destroy, fills them with shame and with a holy horror of self, especially as they imagine that they are consenting to what is going on within them, although in fact they are far from doing so. But God does not place them in a state so humiliating and crucifying to nature until they are far advanced, and their will is, so to speak, confirmed in well-doing by long practice.

Among interior persons, nothing is more real and more common than this state, which is a very mysterious one. And if their director does not understand it, he is liable to make great mistakes, which may cause many of his penitents to despond. These certainly do not wish to sin, and they do all they can not to sin. Yet things escape them which appear to be sinful. They accordingly reproach and accuse themselves of these things as of so many sins; and if their confessor imprudently agrees with them and declares that they have sinned, he would cause them much distress, and they might easily run great risks.

How, then, should the confessor act? He must enter into God's plans, for God wants to destroy self-love in these souls. The confessor must allow them to find no help in themselves, either in the matter of doing good or of avoiding evil. The penitents may insist that they consented, but the confessor must not be too quick to take them at their word. For some time, he will tell them that they have not given their consent; then he may tell them simply to say that they were tried by temptations, without saying they have sinned. He must train them to submit their judgment to his, and to go to Holy Communion in spite of all their repugnances and fears. Such souls are never so pure as when they believe themselves to be covered with sins. Never have they been so humble, so obedient, more dead to their own will and less confident in themselves, as when they are in this state. There are so many marks of God's guidance in their regard that the confessor would have to be very poorly enlightened to doubt them, or unduly timid and irresolute not to recognize them. In such a case, one would be well advised to change one's confessor.

123.   Rom. vii. 19. 22, 23
124.   Rom. vii. 24
125.   Rom. vii. 25
126.   Rom. vii. 17

Twenty-third Maxim: Pure love and hope

*Love is our law: God is our portion; here by faith, in
heaven by sight.*

The Christian law is a law of love. It is all comprised in the
love of God. We are bound to love Him for Himself,
ourselves in Him, and our neighbours for Him. God is the
one principle, from Whom everything flows, and towards
Whom everything must tend. He is the centre in Whom all
things find their unity. Love, says St. Augustine, is the only
worship God exacts, and which alone is pleasing to Him.
Faith alone does not honour God-the devils believe and
tremble. [127] Hope without love is not enough, because it
stops short at God's promises without going on to Himself.
Charity alone reaches Him, is united to Him, and rests in
Him as in the supreme Good. What avails the practice of
exterior works, if they are not animated and quickened by
the heart? Men only pay attention to outward
demonstrations, and they judge the heart by them, for they
cannot see any deeper. But God looks upon the heart. [128]
According to the state of the heart, He appraises all else.

Love is the only thing that makes Our Lord's yoke easy and
His burden light. [129] Fear causes us to feel the whole
weight of the law; hope lightens it but in part; love alone
removes the whole burden of it. According to St.
Augustine, the lover feels nothing burdensome to him, or if
it be a burden, he loves it. The lover counts what he does as
nothing, fears lest he does not enough, and longs ever to do
more. Love knows no bounds, and is always able to grow
stronger, above all if its object be infinitely lovable. To
love such an object is at once a motive and a means to love
it more. The more it is loved, the better is it known; and the
better it is known, the more one longs to love it. In this

way, knowledge and love serve to increase one another indefinitely.

The soul enjoys the true liberty of the children of God, [130] only in so far as it loves. 'Love' says St. Augustine, 'and do what you will'. You would not wish to do anything contrary to love, nor therefore to a law which is itself wholly founded on love. In the same way, St. Paul says that the law is not made for the just. [131] Why does the just man need an external law; he finds all the precepts written in his heart? And not only does he find there the law, but the perfection of the law. Love would not have him stop short at what God commands: it urges him to pass on to those things which please Him, to what He counsels without expressly commanding. Love is his rule, his whole desire, his whole strength. That is why he is perfectly free, for freedom consists in doing what we will, and in willing what we do.

Such love is all the purer, as the heart becomes detached from its own interests and tends towards the object loved, without looking back on itself. This degree of purity is the state to which God is continually striving to raise the soul that has given itself to Him. All the favours which He has bestowed on it, the trials through which He has caused it to pass, the sacrifices He exacts of it, all combine to purify its love, and to separate all alloy from it. Thus may the interior way be defined, not as a state of pure love, but as a constant tending towards it.

It may be said that the tending towards pure love is also the aim of the ordinary Christian, and I agree: but with a distinction. If, in the normal way, retaining our liberty, we mingle our own activity with the workings of grace, this will hinder those workings from producing their full effect.

In the passive way, however, having given to God all right over our own will, God acts upon us more powerfully; nothing hinders or restrains His work, and therefore it achieves its full effect. It is difficult, not to say impossible, for this difference to be understood by those who are not in the passive way, however perfect they may be otherwise. But it is none the less real, and it would be presumptuous to doubt the word of those saints who have spoken on the matter from their own experience.

However, we are not to take fright at the mention of pure love, as though it were contrary to Christian hope. Those who have so written as to give this impression either expressed themselves badly or were misunderstood. In this life, charity does not, and never can, exclude hope. So long as we do not possess the thing we love, we must desire to do so. And not only desire it, but hope for it, in virtue of God's promises. And we count it a duty to hope for it, by reason of the express command which He lays upon all His children.

The love of God is not such as to exclude hope, no matter to what degree it has arrived, but is the actual possession of God or the assurance of possessing Him. The actual possession only takes place in heaven, the assurance in Purgatory. Here on earth, where the enjoyment of God is neither perfect nor assured, and where, apart from a special revelation, one cannot even be sure of one's salvation or that one is in a state of grace, [132] how is it possible for charity to banish hope from the Christian heart? To do so would be to enter on a state of despair absolutely incompatible with love.

In this life, charity always implies the other two theological virtues; and, far from destroying them, perfects them in

perfecting itself. Anything that could destroy faith and hope
in us would all the more destroy charity. It is absurd, then,
to think that the trials that are sent to purify our love can in
any way lessen the virtue of hope. It is equally absurd to
imagine that there can be such a thing as a state, or even an
act, of pure love, which would involve a renouncement of
hope. Even if hope may not be the motive for the love,
nevertheless it exists at the bottom of the heart. In the
words of St. Paul: there remain faith, hope and charity.
[133] This is the case even with the greatest saints, so long
as they are still pilgrims in via. It is only at the end of their
pilgrimage that faith ceases, because one no longer
believes, but sees clearly. Similarly hope comes to an end,
because one either possesses or is assured of possessing. So
charity reigns alone, since in heaven there is scope only for
charity. Such is St. Paul's teaching; a doctrine, incidentally,
based on the very essence and definition of the three
theological virtues.

The fact that God urges certain souls to sacrifices in their
most severe trials, proves nothing to the contrary of what I
have been saying. God's intention is not to purify love at
the expense of hope (for that would be acting contrary to
Himself), but, while purifying love to purify hope at the
same time, and so lead the soul to place God's glory and
will above all selfinterest. This does not require the soul to
renounce its happiness, but to subordinate it, as it must be
subordinated, to God's good pleasure, which must always
be its motive.

It might perhaps have been better not to have touched on
these matters, which are extremely delicate and very
difficult to explain, or even to understand with perfect
precision. It is not necessary that souls should know about
these things in advance, because those whom God calls to

such a great sacrifice are few and far between; and when they are in this state, their perplexity and darkness are such that they could not make use of their previous knowledge, even if they wanted to. As for the directors of such souls, God never fails, provided they consult Him in prayer, to give them the necessary light to guide their penitents, and the best books would be useless to them, if they did not seek that light in their own union with God. But as this subject, which is the highest of all relating to the interior life, caused much public comment at the end of the seventeenth century, and in consequence of a just condemnation many persons became prejudiced against a subject understood by very few, I have thought fit to explain the matter briefly, in order to correct certain false impressions, and to dispel prejudice.

The great and inestimable advantage of love is that it leads to the eternal possession of God: this is the privilege of love alone. Faith and hope cannot open the gate to heaven, unless charity be joined to them. [134] Even during this life, love enables us to possess God to a certain degree, for loving Him is the beginning of possession. We may love any other object without possessing it, or possess it without loving it. But God, Who is the supreme Good, has this peculiar to Himself alone: His love cannot be separated from the possession of Him, nor the possession of Him from His love.

Of course such possession is imperfect on earth, because it is enjoyed beneath the veil of faith. The heart delights in God, and is filled with Him and contemns everything else. If it have yet any desire left, it can only be for a fuller and more assured enjoyment of that love. Yes: when the love of God reaches a certain point, it stills all the agitations of the human heart, even in this life. It brings a peace, which cannot be troubled, so long as the love subsists which gave it birth.

But who are those in whom love rises to such a height as to give them, even in this land of exile, a foretaste of the happiness of their heavenly home? They are souls who may justly be termed children of God, because they are led by His Spirit. [135] As sons, they already share in their Father's inheritance. Others partake of His gifts and graces; these enter already into an anticipated possession of Himself. Having given themselves to God, God gives Himself wholly to them. He unites them with Himself, communicating to them something of that changelessness of peace and rest which He Himself enjoys.

And the proof of this is that no earthly happenings of any kind cause them either joy or sorrow. They accept all things with an even mind, and though some slight agitation may take place on the surface of their souls, the depths of the soul are undisturbed. I have only to appeal to the experience of the saints. Were there ever souls more calm and still? One has only to look at their serenity in the midst of the most painful tortures. Was it the effect of their own reflections or efforts at self-control, made at such moments? Indeed no: they owed it to their possession of God, Who so filled their hearts that there was no room left for any other feeling or thought of self.

127.   James ii. 19
128.   I Kings xvi. 7
129.   Cf. Matt. xi. 30

130.   Cf. Rom. viii. 21
131.   I Tim. i. 9
132.   Cf. Eccles. ix. 1
133.   I Cor. xiii. 13
134.   Cf. I Cor. xiii. 2
135.   Cf. Rom. viii. 14

Twenty-fourth Maxim: Conclusion

Let us pray that these Maxims may redound to the greater glory of God, and the happiness of our own souls.

The words which serve as a heading to this chapter are not in the form of a maxim, but they contain three great truths, with the explanation of which I will close this little work.

The first is that by prayer we may be counted among the number of interior souls; the second, that such souls glorify God more than others; the third, that they are by far the happiest.

I suppose myself addressing one who, having read or heard somewhat concerning the interior life, feels a keen desire to live that divine life. This desire manifestly comes from God, and is itself a beginning of that which it seeks. I would say, then, keep the spark alight by fervent and assiduous prayer. Offer yourself sincerely to God, not just once in a way but every day, and many times a day. Beg Him to open for you the way to the promised land. With that end in view, communicate often, occupy yourself with good works, fulfil the duties of your state, bear bravely with the worries attendant on them, and you will undoubtedly obtain the grace you are asking for. For God does not plant such a desire in a soul, without intending to satisfy it. Should you be eager in the pursuit of this great blessing, know that it is God Who is inspiring you. If you do all that is in your power to obtain it, again it is God Who is the author of your zeal, and is animating and sustaining it. If you persevere in asking for it and do not allow yourself to become discouraged, you will certainly obtain what you seek. For how could God refuse such a request from a soul that longs to be His entirely, and will He not grant it in the measure of the desire He Himself has given?

But you must be careful not to excite your imagination, or become impatient or over-anxious in your quest. Pray quietly, and await quietly the answer to your prayer. God has His own time for answering it: seek not to hurry His work. On the other hand, beware of tepidity, indifference or negligence in your prayer, for that would be a sign that you do not know nor want the grace you are asking for.

If, however, you pray as you should do, God will in due time take possession of your soul, either all at once or by degrees. If the former, you will feel immediately a perfect assurance of it, from the sudden change which will take place in you. If it happens gradually, then follow the workings of grace step by step, and be extremely faithful. Everything depends upon your fidelity. Once introduced into the interior way, you have but to walk in it, directed interiorly by the Holy Spirit, and exteriorly by your spiritual guide.

There are few Christians who do not receive some insight into the interior way. Either they receive it while remaining faithful to the grace of their baptism, or God gives it to them when they sincerely return to Him after wandering away from Him, it may be far and for long periods. If only souls wanted and knew how to cultivate that tiny seed; if directors, themselves interior souls, would take the necessary pains to develop it, the effect of their combined efforts would soon be apparent, and the early steps in the way would not present much difficulty. Most of the trouble arises from the false or imperfect notions we at once begin forming when we enter the interior way, on the strength of which we introduce all sorts of practices, methods and activities, in which there is a great deal of self and self-will. Difficulties also arise through having one's own fixed idea of how God wants to be served, and this hinders the work of grace, a habit which it is almost impossible to throw off once one has arrived at a certain age. They arise also from prejudices one has conceived against the interior life, esteeming it to be dangerous and out of the ordinary, and subject to a thousand illusions. Lastly, difficulties often come from the directors themselves, who for similar reasons, or because they do not want to take the trouble or are afraid to risk their reputation, close the entrance to the interior life to those under their care.

If both penitent and director were actuated by zeal for God's interests, how very differently they would think. For it is certain that we cannot glorify God more than by dedicating ourselves entirely to Him, so that He may lead us as He will. Indeed, it is God Who then glorifies Himself in the soul wherein He finds no resistance. And can we doubt that He glorifies Himself in the best way, according to the whole scope of His designs, when the creature offers no opposition? The will and the means are both within His power: nothing but man's free will can impede the workings of His grace, and the impediment ceases to exist when that liberty is freely yielded up into God's hands.

Moreover, God's glory lies in the free submission of our will to His. If that submission is absolute, extending to everything without exception; if it is continuous and never rescinded, the glory that God derives from it is as great as is possible, for the creature can offer Him nothing greater.

What glorifies God is our sanctification, and the more God acts in a soul by grace, the more that soul is sanctified. In what soul does God act more freely, more efficaciously and

more independently, than in one that has constituted Him
master of its faculties; that keeps these continuously
submissive to His will, only reserving for itself a constant
attention to His guidance, and an exact fidelity in following
it? If it perseveres to the end in this disposition, is it not
clear that God will raise it to that degree of sanctity which
He intends for it, and that He will derive all the glory He
expects from it?

What glorifies God more is when we see Him alone in
everything; when we refer all to Him, look only to His
interests and consider ours as subordinate to His; when,
like Job, we receive good and evil at His hands with an
even mind, and bless His name in all things. But that is just
what an interior soul does. Its eye-that is, its intention--is
single and pure, ever turned towards God; no lower view or
created interest defiles it. Such a soul is in a state of holy
indifference respecting what befalls it. All that it receives
from God is welcome, because sent by Him. It is as
contented to bear all manner of crosses and trials, as it is to
be loaded with good things, for its true and only good is
God's good pleasure.

Last of all, the glory that God derives from these souls in
heaven is proportionate to that which they have given Him
on earth. Then, perfected in love, rapt in the vision of Him
to Whom they gave themselves when as yet they knew Him
only by faith, they will offer Him eternally a tribute of
adoration, thanksgiving, praise and love, which is beyond
all human conception. As their holocaust of themselves
bore a direct resemblance to that of Our Lord, so the Father
will receive from them a special glory of the same kind as
He receives from the sacred humanity of His only-begotten
Son. But the glory rendered by the creature to its Creator is
the rule and measure of its own happiness. Judge, then, if it

be possible, what will be the happiness of such souls in heaven. All I can say is that God will give Himself to them as they gave themselves to Him. They gave themselves to Him without reserve, with the whole of their heart; so, too, God will not be sparing in the reward He gives them. They gave themselves to Him, weak, poor, imperfect creatures; He will give Himself to them as God, infinitely great, infinitely powerful, infinitely rich, generous and glorious. They loved Him as mere creatures, according to the narrow capacity of their hearts; He will love them as God, with a love as far beyond their own as the Uncreated Essence is beyond the being formed out of nothingness. If I may dare to say so, He will be as devoted and consecrated to them as they were to Him. In a word, He will render them all for all; but an All boundless and infinite in return for an all limited and finite. They gave without measure, they will receive without measure; a pure, generous and utterly lavish love will recompense them. Such profusion would, indeed, exhaust the riches of God, were they not inexhaustible. [136] Such is the happiness awaiting these souls in heaven.

That these souls, whilst yet on earth, are happy, so far as the conditions of this life allow, who can doubt? What is happiness but the love and possession of the sovereign Good? These souls love the sovereign Good: even in this life they possess Him according to the full capacity of their heart. God fills the heart, leaving no room for any other desire. Nothing draws them; nothing that the world can offer them in the way of honours, wealth or pleasure attracts them; they are in possession of a happiness that makes them despise all else. And this blessing, does it consist in the gifts and favours and consolations of God? By no means. They receive these things gratefully when it pleases God to send them, but they do not desire them, nor cling to them; nor do they fret when they are deprived of them. The real blessing they possess is God Himself, and He is infinitely greater than all His gifts.

Again, what is happiness? Happiness is peace of heart, and that peace never leaves them: a peace intense, changeless, unaffected by feelings, independent of vicissitudes, both of the natural and supernatural order; abiding in the depth of the heart, despite all trials and temptations, bound up with the very crosses they bear, and without which they would not wish to live. All this is incomprehensible, but it is true.

Would you know whether these souls are happy? Ask them if there is anything in the world that would induce them to wish themselves otherwise situated, to desire any alleviation of their sufferings, to withdraw themselves from the rule of the divine will. Ask them if they even wish God to relieve them and end their pain. They answer No. They will tell you that they are more than content; that all their desires are fulfilled, so long as God is glorified in them as He would wish to be. Show me any other happiness on earth to be compared to theirs--there is none. The happiness of innocence is great; that of penitence also. But the happiness of souls that God sanctifies Himself by the interior way of abandonment and pure faith is greater than them all. One needs to be in it to believe this; but when one has advanced somewhat on the way, there is no longer any doubt.

136.   Cf. Rom. xi. 33

Made in the USA
Monee, IL
23 July 2023

39763914R00138